Evaluation in schools

G000153269

This book provides practical guidance for a school to use in developing its evaluation policy and strategy. It is based on the authors' extensive experience of working with teachers, and draws on the responses of teachers and senior managers in trialling self-evaluation. The book is a stand-alone package for primary and secondary schools containing the materials, information and guidance needed to get started on a structured approach to evaluation. It could also be effectively used with LEA personnel to develop their evaluation skills.

The central focus of the book is the staff development programme outlined in Part II. This provides a comprehensive package ready for use within a school or by a cluster or consortium of schools. The training materials include full objectives, programmes for training days and detailed workshop tasks. These can be photocopied for use by schools wishing to follow the staff development scheme.

In order to support this training package, Part I provides relevant background information, practical guidance and examples of material trialled in schools. Several figures are included which are suitable for use as overhead transparencies or handouts which can be photocopied for use as part of the training process. Part III includes a case study of introducing a whole-school approach to evaluation and moves on to discuss some broader issues which schools may wish to consider in further developing an integrated evaluation system.

Glyn Rogers had a wide range of teaching and management experience in schools and FE colleges prior to his appointment in 1985 as Director of the Dyfed TVEI project, and LEA adviser for 14–19 education. **Linda Badham** had eleven years' teaching and management experience in schools. She was then appointed Assistant Director of the Dyfed TVEI pilot and since January 1991 she has had responsibility for whole curriculum issues at the Curriculum Council for Wales. Both authors have organised, contributed to or have been trainers on numerous courses in aspects of evaluation and other curricular and management issues, at LEA and national level.

Educational Management Series
Edited by Cyril Poster

Evaluation in schools

Getting started on training and implementation

Glyn Rogers and Linda Badham

London and New York

First published 1992
by Routledge
11 New Fetter Lane, London EC4P 4EE

Simultaneously published in the USA and Canada
by Routledge
a division of Routledge, Chapman and Hall, Inc.
29 West 35th Street, New York, NY 10001

© 1992 Glyn Rogers and Linda Badham

Typeset in 10/12pt September by Leaper & Gard Ltd., Bristol
Printed and bound in Great Britain by
Biddles Ltd., Guildford and King's Lynn

British Library Cataloguing in Publication Data
A catalogue record for this title is available from the British Library.

Library of Congress Cataloging in Publication Data
Rogers, Glyn, 1946–
        Evaluation in schools : getting started on training and
    implementation / Glyn Rogers and Linda Badham.
            p. cm. — (Educational management series)
        Includes bibliographical references (p.   ) and index.
        ISBN 0–415–08077–0
        1. Educational evaluation—Great Britain. 2. Teachers—In-service
    training—Great Britain. I. Badham, Linda. II. Title.
    III. Series.
LB2822.75.R64 1992   91-46053
371.1′44—dc20   CIP

Contents

Figures

Key *OHP – overhead projector transparency*
HO – handout

Training materials

Foreword

Amid the welter of innovations from central government in England and Wales, all of which stem directly or indirectly from the requirement that schools and colleges become more accountable, teachers, governors and administrators are crying out for practical guidance. In the field of evaluation, in particular, professional practitioners recognise this need, have some concept of their role, but so far have had little help in establishing processes that are both easily comprehensible and manageable within reasonable constraints of time. Two volumes within the Routledge Education Management Series now offer that help: *Time Constrained Evaluation* by Brian Wilcox, published in 1992, and now this book.

Its authors have considerable experience in the practicalities of school evaluation. Linda Badham, now Director: Whole Curriculum at the Curriculum Council for Wales, formerly Assistant Director of the Dyfed TVEI Pilot Project, and Glyn Rogers, Director of the TVEI Project for Dyfed LEA, have tested out over a period of three years all the materials within this book. As administrators close to the field of action, that is the schools themselves, they are well aware of what can and cannot be done in the limited time available, but also of what must be done in the future to meet the obligations for accountability that are incumbent on schools.

This book contains no tablets of stone. Schools must be able to select what for them is most relevant and to adapt to suit their specific needs. At the same time the following pages contain a broad framework within which every school will easily be able to find its own route to evaluation. The wealth of figures, which schools may use either as they stand or can readily adapt, make this a guide to action which no school, primary or secondary, can afford to be without.

Cyril Poster

Introduction

If you have reached the stage where you feel the need to introduce a systematic approach to evaluation as a normal part of your school's working practices, then this book has you in mind. It aims to provide practical guidance for a school to use in developing its evaluation policy and strategy. It is based on experience and draws on the responses of teachers and senior managers in trialling self-evaluation.

The kernel of the book is the staff development programme described in detail in Part II. This provides a comprehensive package ready for use within a school or by a cluster or consortium of schools. The training materials, listed on p. ix, provide full objectives, programmes for training days and detailed workshop tasks. *These can be photocopied for use by schools wishing to follow the staff development scheme.*

In order to support this training package, Part I provides relevant background information, practical guidance and examples of material trialled in schools. We have included several figures which are suitable for use as overhead projector transparencies and/or handouts. The list of figures provided on pp. vii–viii suggests the most appropriate use for each. *These materials can be photocopied for use as part of the training process.*

Part III includes a case study introducing a whole-school approach to evaluation and moves on to discuss some broader issues which schools may wish to consider in further developing an integrated evaluation system.

Our intention has been to give primary and secondary schools a stand-alone package containing the materials, information and guidance needed to get started on a structured approach to evaluation. In addition, this book could be used with LEA personnel to develop their evaluation skills.

We wish to thank those of our colleagues who worked with us in developing various evaluation instruments during the training conferences and who trialled them in their schools and consortia as part of the Dyfed TVEI programme. Furthermore, we are indebted to 'Dan yr Olwg' School and particularly to G.R. who provided the information that allowed us to write up the case study.

Abbreviations

DES	Department of Education and Science
GCSE	General Certificate of Secondary Education
HMI	Her Majesty's Inspectorate
INSET	In-Service Training
IT	Information Technology
JIIG-CAL	Jobs Ideas and Information Generator – Computer Assisted Learning
LEA	Local Education Authority
LMS	Local Management of Schools
PI	Performance Indicator
TVEI	Technical and Vocational Education Initiative
WO	Welsh Office

National Curriculum subjects

Ar	Art
En	English
Gg	Geography
Hi	History
Ma	Maths
MFL	Modern Foreign Language
Mu	Music
PE	Physical Education
Sc	Science
Te	Technology
We	Welsh

Part I

Evaluation in context

Chapter 1

In defence of evaluation

Evaluation is the process of systematically collecting and analysing information in order to form value judgements based on firm evidence. These judgements are concerned with the extent to which particular targets are being achieved. They should therefore guide decision-making for development.

The term 'evaluation' is sometimes used to refer specifically to the judgemental part of this process only. We have found the broader definition given above more useful, because the validity of the value judgements which can be made is greatly dependent on the nature and provenance of the data collected. In this context, the need is for practicable data collection and handling systems which provide sound evidence on which to base judgements. The primary purpose of this book is to assist schools in the task of embedding such systems in their staff's normal practices.

Evaluation is often set in the context of a monitoring, evaluation and review cycle (Tipple, 1989).

- *Monitoring* is the process of collecting and presenting information in relation to specific objectives on a systematic basis. It should always be undertaken for specific purposes if the effort involved is to be justified.
- *Evaluation* takes this process a stage further in that the information is analysed and value judgements are made.
- *Review* is a considered reflection on progress, using evaluation data to inform decisions for strategic planning.

A simple model showing the interrelationship between these three activities is shown in Figure 1.1. The place of evaluation within a school's management cycle is explored more fully in Chapter 2.

WHY EVALUATE AT ALL?

There are two main purposes for evaluation of performance:

- ACCOUNTABILITY to *prove* quality, for example, to demonstrate that funding is being properly deployed to maintain and improve standards;
- DEVELOPMENT to *improve* quality, for example, to assist in the process of improving curriculum development and delivery.

Figure 1.1 The interrelationship between monitoring, evaluation and review

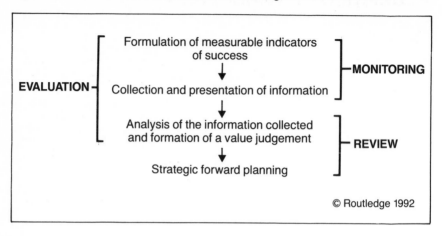

© Routledge 1992

Accountability is a central thread running through most of the changes enshrined in the 1988 Education Reform Act. It has been suggested that the various school-based evaluation initiatives of the late 1970s and 1980s were, in general, disappointing because they seldom functioned as appropriate instruments of accountability (Clift, Nuttall and McCormick, 1987). However, in the present climate, school-based evaluation is more likely to take root because schools now have to provide information about their performance over a wide range of issues, and in some detail, to parents, governors and the LEA, particularly under Local Management of Schools (LMS). With the coming of the Parents' Charter, this accountability is being brought very much to the fore and places an even greater responsibility on schools and their governing bodies, while reducing the role of the LEA.

The primary function of all this accountability is to raise standards. The Parents' Charter states that governors will need to publish an action plan following the report of independent inspectors on the school once every four years. In the period between external inspections, schools will want to monitor the implementation of the action plan and be well prepared to meet the next full inspection. However, a major task facing any school's senior management is that of establishing a climate in which staff view evaluation positively. This is more readily achieved when teachers have been fully consulted about the development plan and have had a major say both in determining the evaluation criteria and in agreeing how the information collected is to be used. In this way, schools can ensure that they have the data they need to aid development, and staff will be less likely to feel under threat from the evaluation. Moreover, where the parameters of the evaluation are not explicit within an agreed development plan, teachers may be uncertain about what precisely are the targets at which their school is aiming. It is less than helpful for them to be told *post factum* that they failed to

Figure 1.2 Purposes of evaluation

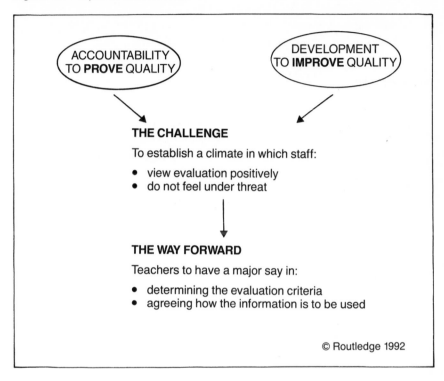

reach these targets – the shifting goal-post syndrome. In sum, evaluation is more effective in raising standards when staff view it as having a developmental as well as an accountability focus. Figure 1.2 summarises these points.

WHY ADOPT A PLANNED APPROACH?

School managers have always had to take important and far-reaching decisions. Traditionally, they could often rely on experience to make these decisions against a familiar and relatively stable backcloth. Nowadays, however, change is the norm and crucial decisions are often required very quickly. Managers need reliable information systems to make sound decisions under changing circumstances.

The principal benefit of using a planned approach to evaluation is that it is designed to provide relevant and reliable information on an ongoing basis to inform strategic forward planning. The planned evaluation is characterised by:

- agreed target areas for evaluation;
- explicitness about criteria for the evaluation of success;

- an evaluation plan which outlines who will collect the data, when, and what will be the source of the information;
- a systematic approach to the collection and recording of information where all involved use appropriate, agreed evaluation instruments.

Features of the traditional and planned approaches to evaluation are contrasted in Figure 1.3.

Figure 1.3 Traditional and planned evaluation contrasted

	TRADITIONAL FEATURES	PLANNED FEATURES
CRITERIA	IDIOSYNCRATIC • Tenuous relationship between evaluation criteria and the policy being evaluated • Performance indicators non-explicit, not shared between parties involved in the activities	EXPLICIT AND AGREED prior to implementation • Specific target areas for evaluation agreed as priorities; evaluation criteria based on objectives as set out in school development plan • Performance indicators formulated and agreed at the planning stage
EVALUATION PLAN	AD HOC • No explicit time-scale • Who does what: unclear • Fitted in when possible • Link with policy not clear • Undemanding in terms of preparation	STRUCTURED • Agreed time-scale • Who does what: documented • Part of the development planning cycle • Explicit links with aims and objectives • Requires detailed planning
METHODS	IMPRESSIONISTIC • Source determined by what/ who is available • 'Lucky dip' sample used • Evaluation questions and methods rarely thought out systematically • Lack of consistency in approach • Analysis of data an afterthought	SYSTEMATIC • Source of information detailed • Representative sample used • Evaluation instruments appropriate for the methods used for data collection • Consistency in criteria and methodology • Systems for recording and analysing information

© Routledge 1992

Source: Based on an original formulation by Dr Colin Morgan, Open University.

CONSTRAINTS

School-based evaluation can only succeed if it does not take up disproportionate amounts of time, effort and resources. Constraints on schools include shortage of time, lack of expertise in evaluation, and reluctance of staff to embrace evaluation as an integral part of normal practice. The following list of suggestions is offered to help ameliorate these problems:

- *Limit the evaluation to a few specific focuses.* Target on some specific, priority objectives which are achievable in the short term and are readily measured, rather than go for the grand plan in a single leap. For example, to increase staff and student use of IT in the National Curriculum core subjects in Years 7 and 8 is a focus for short-term development which is achievable and measurable. By contrast, to improve the quality of IT experiences for all pupils is a laudable aim but one which requires a longer time-span to achieve. Moreover, it would be difficult to measure, needing a level of sophistication in evaluation techniques which few schools would wish to contemplate.

- *Collect essential information only.* Be clear about what information is really necessary for the purposes of evaluation. It is all too easy to be carried away by enthusiasm and to try to collect everything under the sun about the chosen topic when a much more limited exercise would suffice.

- *Make the maximum use of information already available.* Before rushing into designing questionnaires, interview schedules and classroom observation checklists, scan existing sources of information such as attendance registers, room/equipment usage logs, published statistics and other data collected recently by the school. Also make maximum use of any evaluation data about the school, for example, HMI or LEA reports, and TVEI evaluation exercises.

- *Keep it short and simple (KISS).* If you are obliged to gather information from staff or pupils, make your questionnaire/interview brief and unambiguous. Ask only for the information you really need. Avoid questionnaire/interview design requiring complex and time-consuming analysis techniques. Before you collect the data, decide how you will analyse the responses.

- *Make it worthwhile and credible for staff.* Involve staff at an early stage in agreeing the priorities for both development and evaluation in advance. The purposes of the evaluation should then be clear and its potential value to staff in their work and concerns be explicit. The uses of the data – who has access to the information and why – also need to be agreed. Finally, the credibility of the evaluation system within a school has to be established by ensuring that:

  - the outcomes are VALUABLE to all the parties concerned;
  - the judgements made must be VALID, that is they must be supported by evidence;
  - the process should be VERIFIABLE, that is, reasons for the judgements

should be specific with the supporting evidence presented;
- the process should be VIABLE, that is, cost-effective in terms of time and resources and therefore sustainable.

Figure 1.4 summarises these ways of trying to ameliorate the constraints.

Figure 1.4 Possible ways of overcoming the evaluation constraints

---

- Limit the evaluation to a few specific focuses
- Collect essential information only
- Make the maximum use of information already available
- Keep it short and simple (KISS)
- Make it worthwhile and credible for staff

© Routledge 1992

WHICH EVALUATION MODEL?

There are three critical parameters in evaluation:

- the choice of target areas and evaluation criteria;
- the control of the evaluation instruments, including data collection methods;
- the judgement of outcomes.

Figure 1.5 illustrates these three parameters and Figure 1.6 shows the range for each parameter.

The first parameter concerns how the target areas are chosen and the criteria for evaluation are set. At one extreme, these are imposed on the school by someone else. At the other, schools set their own target areas and criteria.

The second parameter deals with control of the evaluation instruments. At one extreme, the instruments, including data collection methods, are determined by an external evaluator. At the other, the school being evaluated chooses which evaluation instruments to use and how to collect the data.

The last parameter is about control of the evaluation outcomes and ranges from a closed to a negotiated judgement. A closed judgement is one where those being evaluated have no part in preparing the final evaluation statement. A negotiated judgement is one where those being evaluated have some influence on the preparation and even the content of the final statement.

Based on these three parameters, we can characterise eight evaluation models, shown in Figure 1.7 and described below. Each model is numbered, its character-istics determining its place in the cube. For example, the traditional HMI inspection model, labelled Model 1, is located in the bottom front left position because all aspects of the evaluation are controlled by the external agent. A full description of each model is given below.

Figure 1.5 Critical parameters in evaluation

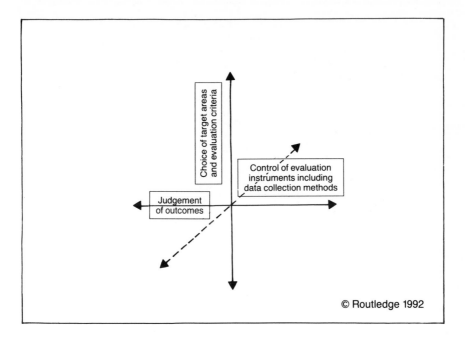

Figure 1.6 Range of each critical parameter in evaluation

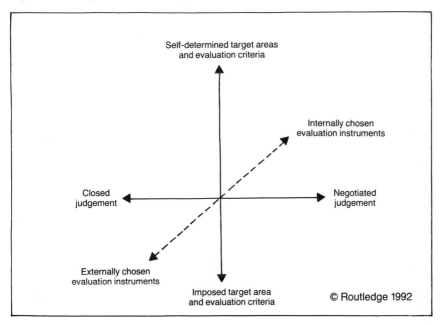

Figure 1.7 Evaluation models

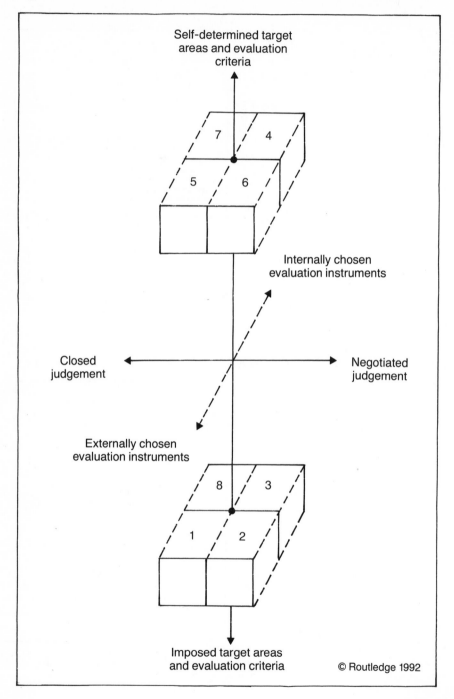

Self-determined target
areas and evaluation
criteria

7   4

5   6

Internally chosen
evaluation instruments

Closed
judgement

Negotiated
judgement

Externally chosen
evaluation instruments

8   3

1   2

Imposed target areas
and evaluation criteria

© Routledge 1992

Model 1   Currently the HMI inspection report, and in the future, the new independent inspectors' report. The criteria, information collected and the judgements made are *all* controlled by the external agencies.

Model 2   The LEA inspection report in its current form. The criteria and evaluation instruments are determined by the inspectors but the final report is negotiated between LEA inspectors and the school. This may not apply in future where LEA personnel function as independent inspectors.

Model 3   Self-evaluation using national or LEA criteria. The criteria are determined by external bodies including currently the LEA, TVEI, and the Curriculum Councils, but increasingly in the future, these criteria will be determined by the new HMI. The school nevertheless chooses which evaluation instruments to use and how to collect the data, and then makes its own judgements.

Model 4   Internal evaluation: all aspects are in the school's control.

Models 5 and 6   External evaluation: in both cases the school determines what is to be evaluated but buys in an expert to undertake the work. In Model 5 the external evaluator has total control over the report whereas in Model 6 the report is negotiated.

Models 7 and 8   Unattractive scenarios: in both cases the school is judged by external arbiters without having had the benefit of their expertise in the planning and execution of the data collection.

Our aim in outlining these various evaluation models is to clarify the range of options available to schools. As suggested earlier, managers need access to relevant and reliable information as the basis for taking informed decisions in rapidly changing circumstances. Certainly they will need to make use of inspection reports (Models 1 and 2), but these will not be sufficiently frequent to provide all the information that managers need. Schools should therefore consider Models 3, 4, 5 and 6. Using an external evaluator (Models 5 and 6) can prove expensive but may be considered worthwhile on occasion, particularly if the expertise of the school's staff can be developed by working with the external consultant. None the less, self-evaluation and internal evaluation (Models 3 and 4) are much more suited to integration in the annual management cycle of the school. This book sets out to prepare staff to operate Models 3 and 4.

Chapter 2

Evaluation within the management cycle

Because a number of technical terms are used in evaluation, we have provided a list of definitions. You may at this stage wish to scan through these definitions and refer back to them as and when you need.

DEFINITIONS

Aim

An aim is a general statement of intention that outlines the ultimate goal without specifying the stages by which it could be achieved. It is important to distinguish between aims and the objectives. The latter term defines the stages through which the aims can be achieved. For example, your aim might be to encourage children to make wise and informed curriculum and career choices. One objective which contributes towards meeting this aim might be to provide a planned careers programme in Years 10 and 11 which integrates the work of teachers and careers officers.

Objective

An objective is a statement of intention that outlines in precise terms a short-term goal which is relevant to achieving the aim. While aims are fairly broad, objectives need to be quite specific. Each should be a clear, concise statement of what is to be achieved.

The development of objectives should, whenever possible, involve agreement by all those concerned, whether they are governors, staff or outside agencies. Such consultation will also help to ensure that the targets set by the objectives are at a level which is achievable. If not, there will be disenchantment because those who have formulated the objectives will be viewed as being out of touch with reality. Worse still, the targets may not be met because the people who are supposed to implement the objectives do not fully appreciate what the school expects from them. Objectives should be measurable so that the school can tell whether or not they are being achieved.

The other important factor to consider is the time-scale over which the objectives are to be achieved. This should be explicit and agreed so that those involved will be clear about when implementation is to take place.

To use an acronym which will be familiar to some readers, objectives should be:

S	pecific
M	easurable
A	greed and achievable
R	elevant
T	imed

Strategy

A strategy is a plan outlining how a specific objective or a series of objectives will be achieved. It indicates what is to be done – how, by whom and when. For example, a school might have the specific objective: within the next academic year to increase from 10 per cent to 25 per cent the number of teachers who have experienced a work placement. The strategy would specify how teachers would be identified, when the placements could occur and with which employers, who would undertake all the necessary organisation, how the financial and resource implications would be met.

In the context of evaluation, the strategy will outline what information is to be collected; how, by whom, and when.

Development plan

The development plan is a statement of priorities to be addressed within a specific period of time. Such plans can be prepared at various levels – LEA, school, department, individual – and should set out common and consistent aims, objectives and strategies. Ideally they should also include evaluation plans.

Performance indicators (PIs)

Performance indicators are the signals of success which will be used to indicate whether the objectives have been achieved. A performance indicator:

- is an indication of the extent of progress made in one area and is not an absolute or general measure of performance;
- should be viewed alongside other evaluation evidence in order to identify

and understand the overall progress achieved;

- should not be used in isolation but as part of an overall system of planning, evaluation and review;
- should be capable of collection over a period of time on a constant basis;
- should be relevant to the objective;
- may be quantitative or qualitative. A quantitative PI is generally used to measure fact rather than opinion, for example, the percentage of Year 2 pupils attaining level 2 or better in their National Curriculum subjects at the end of key stage 1. A qualitative PI attempts to obtain a measure of an attitude or perception, for example, the degree of parental satisfaction with the arrangements for pupil transition between primary and secondary school. Obtaining credible and reliable measures for this second type of PI is much more complex and difficult.

Evaluation instrument

An evaluation instrument is a tool which specifies:

- what information needs to be collected including, where appropriate, lists of questions to be asked;
- what is the source of the information;
- the format for recording the information.

For standardised usage, for example, by a team of evaluators, it may also include guidelines on the analysis of the information. Examples are provided in Chapter 3.

Review

The review involves considered reflection on the progress of the past year's development plan. The consideration of the evaluation information collected should lead to informed value judgements. These will be concerned both with the success of the strategies in delivering these objectives, and also with whether the objectives are indeed contributing to the achievement of the long-term aims. This review will inevitably lead into the following year's strategic forward planning.

THE EVALUATION PLANNING TRIANGLE

In planning evaluation, three interrelated aspects have to be specified, namely objectives, performance indicators and evaluation instruments.

PIs and objectives

Performance indicators are signals of success. They are not general questions or statements in a checklist or audit. Consider the following example:

Incidence of special educational need/learning difficulties including any
provision made for pupils with statements

(DES, 1989a, No. 17)

This is not a PI because it gives no indication of how successful a school is in
supporting pupils with learning difficulties. It certainly highlights a broad issue
which concerns most schools, but it begs the question of what might give a
specific signal either that a school's provision for pupils with special educational
needs was worthwhile or that there was improvement from the previous state.
This question is very difficult to answer without reference to some specific target
or objective.

Suppose that a secondary school had decided to focus on its special
educational needs provision. At an early stage in implementing a new or revised
policy the school might concentrate on encouraging all departments to look
afresh at their planning. One possible objective would be: to produce schemes of
work for Year 10 in all subjects through consultation between subject staff and
members of the special education needs support team. A suitable PI to measure
the success of this objective would be: the number of subject areas which have
revised their schemes of work for Year 10 in consultation with the special needs
support team. Clearly, the limited objective and its associated PI do not deal with
the quality of the pupils' learning experiences. The focus is targeted on the
planning process for developing suitable schemes of work. Later in the implementation of the new or revised policy, the school might wish to have some
measure of the effectiveness of that policy. One possible outcome indicator
would be: the percentage of pupils with special educational needs who gain
external accreditation during Year 11, since an increase in this percentage would
be one – but not the only – possible signal that the policy was indeed improving
pupils' learning experiences. It must be remembered that one signal should be
considered in conjunction with other information before a value judgement can
be made with some degree of confidence.

The examples above are intended to show that PIs are meaningful when they
are derived from specific targets or objectives, whether set by the school, the LEA
or nationally.

PIs and evaluation instruments

Even when PIs are linked with aims and specific objectives, they can be open to a
variety of interpretations. The evaluation instrument provides opportunities for
detailing specific questions which elicit meaningful responses.

Suppose one objective for a secondary or primary school was: to strengthen
and increase the number of links between the school's curriculum and the world
of work. A possible PI would be: number of departments/year teams making use
of links with the world of work in their teaching. The evaluation instrument
would need to ask questions in such a way as to clarify what counted as a link
with the world of work. Thus heads of department/year teams might be asked:

Which of the following links with the world of work has your department/year team established? Please tick the relevant boxes.	
Pupil projects involving local business/industries/ organisations	
Pupil visits to business/industry/other workplace	
Use of pupils' work placement experience in lessons (*secondary schools only*)	
External speakers/consultants whose contributions are relevant to National Curriculum programmes of study	
Teacher-placement involving departmental/year team member(s)	
Other: please specify	

For a small primary school, these questions could be modified so as to apply to each class teacher.

Sometimes, attempting to design an evaluation instrument throws up so many problems that there may be need to reconsider the PI. Within the constraints that schools face, a PI which is extremely difficult to measure is not well suited to self-evaluation. For example, a school might wish to measure the incidence of pupils' exercise of initiative and acceptance of responsibility (DES 1989a, No. 40). However, a high level of expertise and experience is required to design an instrument suitable for obtaining a reliable measure of such a qualitative PI. A school might therefore feel the need to employ a professional evaluator. Alternatively, the school might consider modifying the PI to measure one or two specific examples of pupils' behaviour. For example, the percentage of pupils in a particular year group who submit homework and coursework regularly and on time is measurable; it gives one indication of pupils' acceptance of responsibility and requires only a relatively simple evaluation instrument.

Evaluation instruments and objectives

Similarly, designing the evaluation instruments may throw up problems, not just with PIs, but with the objectives themselves. Sometimes it becomes clear that a given objective is too wide-ranging and ambitious to be achievable in the short term. Also, a group of people working together to design an evaluation instrument may realise that the objective will be open to different interpretations by the staff involved in its implementation. In both cases, the process of evaluation instrument design will have highlighted the need to refine the objective.

In sum, planning evaluation starts with objectives, from which PIs can be formulated; but the planning is not complete until the evaluation instruments to collect the information have been designed. This process is not a simple progression, since designing the evaluation instrument often highlights the need to refine the objective, to make it more specific or less ambiguous. The PI would then be modified accordingly. The three elements are closely interrelated, as illustrated in Figure 2.1.

LINKING DEVELOPMENT PLANS AND EVALUATION

The Education Reform Act and a number of other recent curriculum and organisational initiatives require the use of school development plans in one form or another. The management cycle of planning, implementation and review is familiar to most schools. The next logical step is to integrate evaluation into this cycle. Evaluation should be seen as a coherent element of the established management cycle and not as an isolated or intermittent option. Figure 2.2 sets out the sequence of the overall cycle and shows evaluation as an integral and ongoing feature of the curriculum development process.

Figure 2.1 Evaluation planning triangle

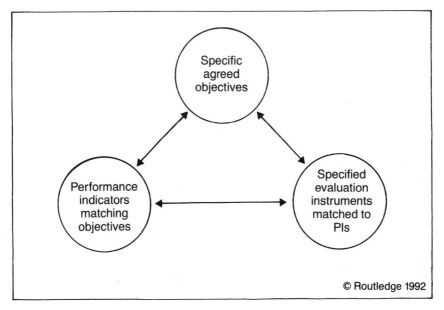

© Routledge 1992

Figure 2.2 The planning, implementation and review cycle

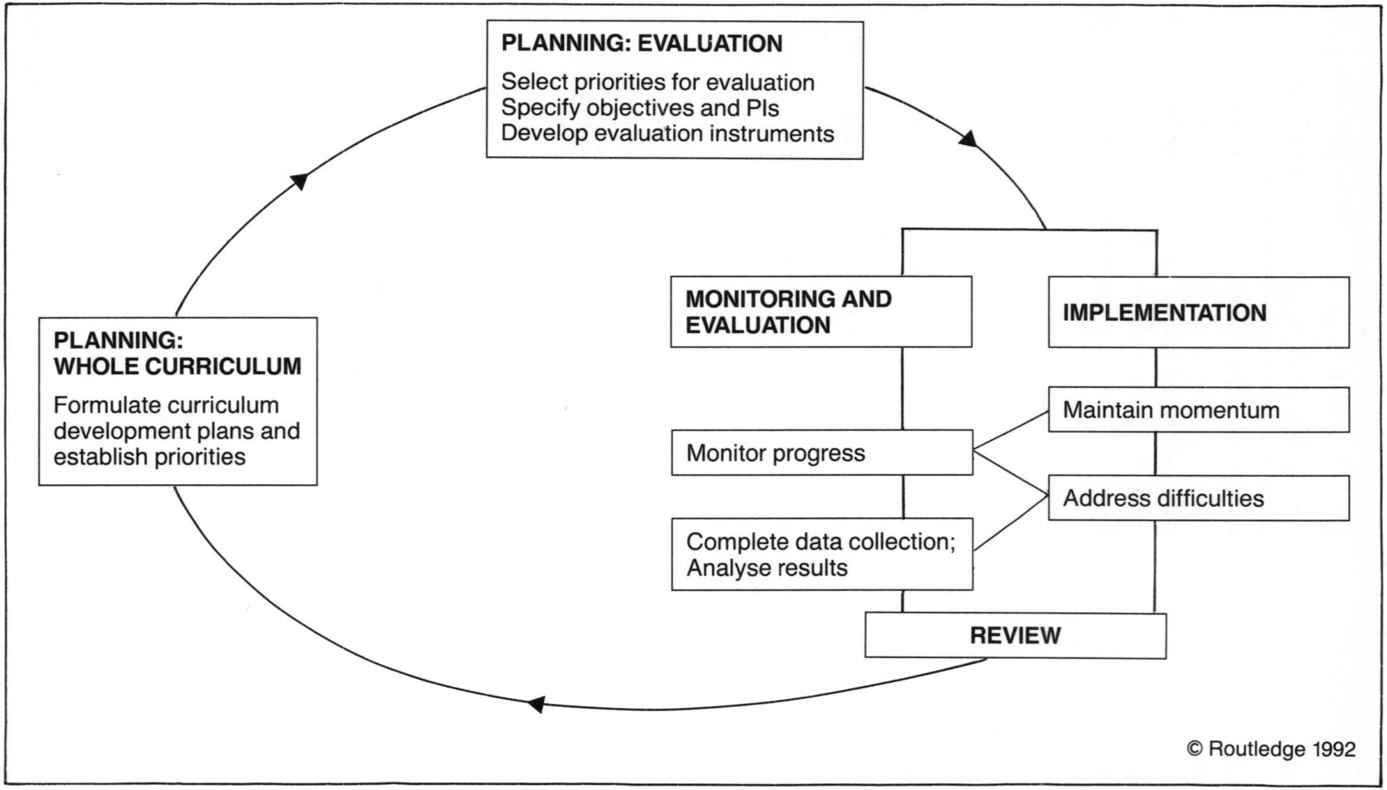

PLANNING: EVALUATION

Select priorities for evaluation
Specify objectives and PIs
Develop evaluation instruments

IMPLEMENTATION

Maintain momentum

Address difficulties

MONITORING AND EVALUATION

Monitor progress

Complete data collection;
Analyse results

REVIEW

**PLANNING:
WHOLE CURRICULUM**

Formulate curriculum
development plans and
establish priorities

© Routledge 1992

In order to ensure that evaluation does not become a bolt-on activity, it is important to consider its implication at each stage of the cycle.

Planning stage

Planning should not stop at deciding what the school's priorities for development are and how to achieve them. It is important to think out how to recognise whether or not the plan is working. The evaluation needs to be planned as early as possible. Indeed, planning the evaluation often helps to clarify the thinking as to what action is required to achieve a given target. The various steps in the planning process are presented in Figure 2.3.

Figure 2.3 Steps in planning which include the planning of evaluation

QUESTIONS	PLANNING RESPONSE
What do we wish to achieve?	Determine overall aims
How will this be achieved?	Define objectives and determine the associated strategies
What should we evaluate?	Decide on priorities/target areas for evaluation
What would count as evidence of success?	Establish performance indicators
What are the sources of the information and how will we collect the information? What specific information is required to help form a value judgement?	Decide where the information can be obtained and how to acquire it Decide on the specific information to be collected and the format for recording } Design evaluation instruments
How will we use the information collected?	Determine: • how to analyse the data • how to present the data • who will have access to the findings © Routledge 1992

Implementation and the formative evaluation stage

There is a tendency for guidelines on school development plans to describe implementation and evaluation as separate phases. In some ways this is understandable, since checking on progress logically follows implementation. However, there is a risk that schools will consider the requirements of evaluation only late in the cycle and therefore lose some of the benefits.

It is desirable to treat the processes of implementation and evaluation as interwoven, not as a period of implementation followed by a separate intense period of evaluation at the end. When implementation and evaluation are integrated and ongoing, evaluation can help to shape and guide the strategies employed. Suppose, for example, that a school had decided to integrate children with special needs into mainstream classes. It would be very necessary to monitor – throughout the year, and not just at the end – the children's progress and the effectiveness of the support strategies for them. This would provide opportunities for addressing difficulties early enough to benefit these particular children.

One way to support integration of implementation and evaluation is to develop the evaluation instruments prior to implementation and to agree an appropriate timetable for data collection. Clearly, the constraints of time will allow for only limited monitoring during the implementation phase. But, as the example above illustrates, dipstick exercises during the year can be beneficial, even though the major collection of data will occur once, prior to the review.

REVIEW

The relationship between evaluation, review and strategic planning

We have defined 'review' as a considered reflection on the progress of the previous year's development plan. This considered reflection should be such as to provide structured opportunities for all the relevant personnel to meet, discuss and reach agreement. The discussion should use all the available evaluation data to arrive at shared value judgements on:

- whether the objectives set out in the strategic plan have been met;
- the extent to which those objectives are contributing to achieving the broad aims;
- the action required in the light of this.

It is important to remember that the purpose of the review is not simply to point up failures. Recognition of success is essential both to maintain and improve staff morale and to disseminate proven examples of good practice. A wider knowledge of such practice is needed if the positive lessons which have been learned are to be extended to other aspects of school life. Nevertheless, there will be instances where the school has not achieved all it would have wished. Review gives an opportunity for constructive analysis of the difficulties so as to formulate a strategy for future action.

Figure 2.4 Evaluation, review and forward planning

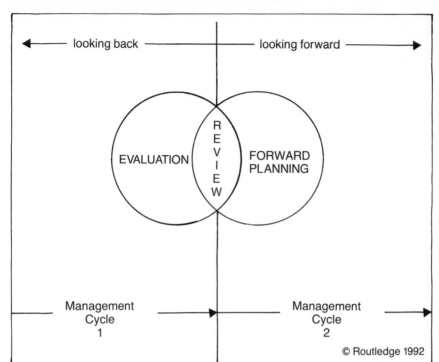

Inevitably, the review process leads into planning for the next cycle. This planning will range beyond ongoing activities to a consideration of new priorities for development. The relationship between evaluation, review and planning is illustrated diagrammatically in Figure 2.4. Review can be seen as linking the evaluation of the present situation with the strategic planning for the next phase.

The term 'review' is often used much more loosely than as illustrated above, to refer to the general notion of looking back and taking stock. We recommend the more structured concept associated with a summative review, as illustrated in Figure 2.5, since the process of review is of greatest value where:

- reflection is based on sound evidence;
- value judgements are agreed by all key personnel;
- action follows as a result.

Review in school

The involvement of all key personnel is the cornerstone to using the review effectively. In a small primary school, the whole staff could be involved together. In larger primary and in secondary schools, this may not be feasible, both in

Figure 2.5 Tasks undertaken in the review

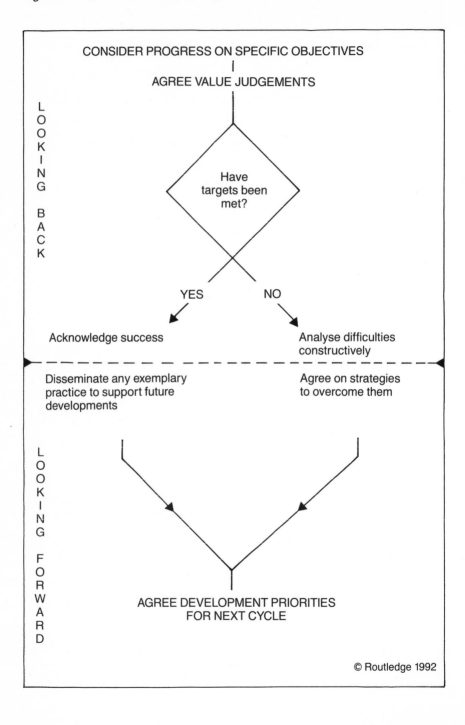

CONSIDER PROGRESS ON SPECIFIC OBJECTIVES

AGREE VALUE JUDGEMENTS

LOOKING BACK

Have targets been met?

YES   NO

Acknowledge success   Analyse difficulties constructively

Disseminate any exemplary practice to support future developments   Agree on strategies to overcome them

LOOKING FORWARD

AGREE DEVELOPMENT PRIORITIES FOR NEXT CYCLE

© Routledge 1992

Figure 2.6 School evaluation ethics statement

- The nature and purpose of any questionnaire, interviews or observations to be undertaken during evaluation will be made clear in advance to the staff concerned.

- The use of any data collected from individual staff or pupils will be guided by the principle of CONFIDENTIALITY. This will mean that, in any report material, whether verbal or written, the author(s) will ensure that no pupils or staff are identified by name in the context of a value judgement. In addition, no quotations will be attributed to their makers, without their consent.

- Staff will have the right to read and comment on accounts which, although not identifying them, portray their work and concerns.

- The senior management team will have the right to retain any potentially sensitive data relating to individuals. In such circumstances, the headteacher may be expected to provide an analysis of the data, safeguarding the anonymity of individual staff or pupils for the purposes of the establishment annual review.

- Prior to review, staff will be apprised of the criteria determining who will attend any given review meeting.

© Routledge 1992

terms of the number of people involved and because detailed discussion of, for example, subject-related issues is not appropriate to members of other faculties or departments. Nevertheless, review should be a whole-school activity. One possible scenario for achieving this in a secondary school is given below.

- Senior managers meet to agree on the priorities which the whole-school review should address and, in broad terms, to decide what the school wants out of the review.
- Faculty/department/curricular area reviews consider, with guidance from a senior manager, issues relevant to their work. The outcomes of these reviews will feed into the whole-school formal review.
- Senior and middle managers meet to undertake the formal whole-school review. This may involve LEA personnel in a partnership approach.
- The outcomes of the whole-school review are communicated to all staff and presented and discussed with governors.

INFORMATION ACCESS AND USE

Evaluation and review can be seen as potentially threatening. A clear ethics statement can help to allay fears and protect individuals from misuse of information about their work and concerns. Such a statement should make explicit:

- why and how the data will be collected;
- a principle of confidentiality in respect of data collected;
- the right of staff to read any accounts relating to their work and concerns;
- who has access to the raw data, particularly where these may be sensitive, and how the rights of individuals will be safeguarded, including their rights under the Data Protection Act of 1984;
- criteria for including various personnel at the review meeting(s).

Figure 2.6 is an example of an ethics statement designed to be used in a school.

Chapter 3

Designing and using evaluation instruments

There is a vast literature devoted to the design and use of evaluation instruments and a wealth of experience to complement it. Our aim in this chapter is to provide a starter pack with enough guidance to help a school set up a limited trialling. We have, however, included a list of sources for further reading which provides a more comprehensive overview for those wishing to pursue this topic in greater depth.

DESIGNING EVALUATION INSTRUMENTS – A SYSTEMATIC APPROACH

Within an LEA or a school, a number of different teachers may well be involved in preparing, trialling and defining evaluation instruments. It is crucial therefore to use a common, agreed framework which:

- ensures that those designing the evaluation instruments keep the aims, objectives and their associated performance indicators in focus throughout the process, as it is all too easy to get side-tracked;
- encourages all those involved in evaluation instrument design to follow a similar process by using a common format;
- sets a standardised pattern for the instruments which facilitates their use by a wider range of staff than those involved in their design.

The proforma illustrated in Figure 3.1 suggests one means of designing suitable evaluation instruments. Before using the proforma, the school will have identified which curricular areas are the targets for evaluation. The proforma is framed so as to start with these priority aims and objectives, using a fresh sheet for each separate objective. The performance indicators are then written in the light of each specific objective. Next it is advisable to decide which information source(s) will provide the measure of success. Details of what information to collect should be structured with the source(s) in mind. In practice, as we indicated in Chapter 2, the process is rarely linear. Each stage often raises queries about earlier decisions so that, for example, framing evaluation questions may force a redefinition of the performance indicator or clarification of the objective.

Figure 3.1 Evaluation planning proforma

Date completed	**Sheet No.** ....

Aim   **Specific Objective**

....

....

KEY STAGE	1	2	3	4	16+
PLEASE ✔					

Performance Indicator	**Information to be collected**
Information Source (Where the information can be obtained and how to acquire it.)	
	© Routledge 1992

In the next three sections we examine in greater depth issues related to sources of information and data collection methods, framing evaluation questions, and the analysis and use of data. However, at this stage an example of evaluation instrument design may be helpful to illustrate the use of the proforma. This example was produced in the first year of trialling self-evaluation by a group of secondary schools.

The schools wished to evaluate the aim: to promote the use of IT across the curriculum. Specifically, the objective was: to increase staff and pupil use of IT in the National Curriculum subjects in Year 10. Three performance indicators (PIs) were identified:

PI1: amount of curricular time for which hardware is in use

Clearly, using the hardware was a necessary condition for delivering IT and low usage would be a cause for concern.

PI2: type of software used in each subject area

This indicator presumed that the schools had a policy on which types of software were appropriate for use in each subject area, and wished to monitor what was actually being used.

PI3: pupil perception of computer usage in each subject area and overall

This indicator focused on the impact IT was having on pupils. The data collected allowed staff to compare pupils' recall of their experiences with what their teachers knew they had provided. It was a first tentative step towards measuring the quality of learning experiences.

In order to evaluate the extent to which the objective of *increasing* staff and pupil use of IT was being met, the data were collected more than once, both within an annual cycle and over two or more years.

The evaluation planning proformas and the use schools made of them are described in the sections that follow. In each case, the timing and administration of the data collection are discussed. Although these evaluation instruments were written for and trialled in secondary schools, suggestions are made for modifying them where necessary to make them suitable for use in primary schools. Finally, we describe some uses which were made of the data collected. Some of the schools involved in trialling used cycles other than the standard five-day week. These schools modified the proformas as appropriate, wherever the term 'week' appeared.

Figure 3.2 Evaluation planning proforma IT1

Date completed	Sheet No. IT1............

Aim	**Specific Objective**
To promote the use of IT across the curriculum	To increase staff and student use in the National Curriculum subjects in Year 10

KEY STAGE	1	2	3	4	16+
PLEASE ✔				✔	

Performance Indicator	**Information to be collected**			
1 Amount of curricular time for which hardware is in use.	How often are your computers used? Please complete one entry for each room which houses one or more curriculum computers.			
	Room designation*	No. of computers	Type(s)	Periods used/week (on average)
Information Source (Where the information can be obtained and how to acquire it.)				
IT equipment usage logs. Returns to be made by all teachers with responsibility for a room containing one or more computer. Results to be collated by senior managers and recorded in the table provided.				
	*If rooms are sharing a computer, e.g. on a trolley, please count only once and bracket relevant rooms.			

Sheet IT1

Figure 3.2 shows evaluation proformas labelled IT1 for PI1. This information was best obtained from IT equipment usage logs during an agreed time-span, for example weeks 3, 4 and 5 of each term. This allowed an average usage in teaching periods per week to be calculated. The choice of mid-term weeks was deliberate in order to avoid data collection during examinations or other times where normal teaching was disrupted. Also, collection during each term gave a more reliable overall picture of normal teaching practice than could have been achieved in a one-off collection.

Where computer usage logs were in normal use, collecting this information was minimally disruptive. Where such logs did not exist, staff needed to introduce them for the specified weeks. Individual teachers handed in their completed logs, immediately after the data collection weeks, to the appropriate senior manager who used them to compile the summary table shown in Figure 3.2. The school was then able to assess the extent to which computing equipment was being used and follow up any areas of concern.

This evaluation instrument focused on individual classrooms and was not restricted to usage by Year 10 pupils. The information collected was used principally to inform judgement on where new computers should be located or existing equipment relocated. However, in many schools, individual teachers spend much of the teaching time in their base-rooms. Hence it was possible in some cases to use the information collected to inform judgements on staff development needs and to identify teaching groups which needed supplementary IT provision. It was also possible to cross-refer inferences drawn from this source with information collected from staff and students on sheets IT2 and IT3 described below.

Sheet IT2

Figure 3.3 shows the evaluation proforma labelled IT2 for PI2. It was designed as a summative evaluation proforma, to be used once yearly. It presumed that the school had a written policy on IT which defined the types of software appropriate for each key stage in each National Curriculum subject. The secondary schools which trialled this instrument were organised in subject-based departments. Schools with different structures, particularly primary schools, could use a modified version of this instrument. The vertical columns would need to reflect the school's internal structure. For example, primary schools could analyse the types of software in use for each year group of pupils.

In the secondary schools which trialled this instrument, the IT co-ordinator consulted each head of department to ascertain what software was being used and the frequency of use. S/he was then able to compile the summary chart shown in Figure 3.3. Although this exercise was demanding on the IT co-ordinator's time, there were benefits. The individual conversations raised heads of departments' awareness of the software available and helped increase their

Figure 3.3 Evaluation planning proforma IT2

Date completed	Sheet No. IT2 ....

Aim
To promote the use of IT across the curriculum

Specific Objective
To increase staff and student use in the National Curriculum subjects in Year 10

KEY STAGE	1	2	3	4	16+
PLEASE ✔				✔	

Performance Indicator	**Information to be collected**
2 Type of software used in each subject area.	Please fill in the table to show how frequently (on a scale of 0 to 3) each type of software is used in each subject area Key: 0 – no use 1 – at least once in term 2 – at least once a month 3 – at least once a week

SUBJECT / SOFTWARE*	En	We +	Ma	Sc	DT	Hi	Gg	MFL	PE
COMMUNICATION									
DATA HANDLING									
CALCULATION									
DESIGN									
CONTROL AND MEASUREMENT									

Information Source
(Where the information can be obtained and how to acquire it.)

Heads of departments, in consultation with IT co-ordinator to complete the table provided.

+ For Schools in Wales   © Routledge 1992

understanding of their particular school's IT policy. If a primary school were to use a modified version of this instrument, the appropriate curriculum co-ordinator should consult individual teachers.

The principal use of the information collected was to monitor the implementation of the school's IT policy. It enabled the IT coordinator to assess what the development needs of individual departments were, to identify overall software and hardware deficiencies, and to bring these to the attention of the senior management.

Sheet IT 3

Figure 3.4 shows the evaluation proforma labelled IT3 for PI3. It involved data collection in secondary schools from pupils via form tutors during the normal pastoral period to minimise disruption. The instrument was designed to be used towards the end of each term so as to chart pupils' experience during the year, rather than undertaking one single summative review. Smaller schools tended to question all the pupils in the year group, while larger schools used a selected sample. In some schools, the experience of the first data collection was used to improve either the questionnaire or the method of administration, or indeed both. A case study of one secondary school's experience of collecting data from pupils is detailed in Part III on pages 78–83.

The pupil questionnaire provided in IT3 is not readily modified for use in primary schools. If pupil data are required, for younger children one-to-one conversations or group discussions are needed to collect information about their perceptions of IT. These could be undertaken by the headteacher, using a semi-structured interview schedule.

Whereas on sheets IT1 and IT2, a matrix to collate information is provided, IT3 gives a pupil questionnaire. Hence, to assist senior managers collate the statistical returns from pupils, responses to questions (a) and (b) of IT3, an analysis sheet was provided. This is shown in Figure 3.5. Since question (c) was open-ended, the categories for analysis purposes would be determined by the nature and indeed the number of responses. Hence no proforma was supplied.

Schools recognised that data collected from pupils' recall would not be definitive. None the less, this information gave pointers to the following:

- subject areas where IT appeared to be having little impact;
- teaching groups which appeared to be experiencing little or no IT.

Senior managers used these data to identify areas of possible concern for further enquiry. In many cases, it was possible to cross-refer data collected from pupils with information obtained from staff and IT equipment usage logs to create a fuller picture.

Having outlined the use of the evaluation planning proforma, we need now to look in greater depth at issues relating to information sources and data collection methods, to framing evaluation questions, and finally to the analysis and use of the data collected.

Figure 3.4 Evaluation planning proforma IT3

Date completed	**Sheet No.** IT3..............

Aim

To promote the use of IT
across the curriculum

Specific Objective

To increase staff and student use in the
National Curriculum subjects in Year 10

KEY STAGE	1	2	3	4	16+
PLEASE ✔				✔	

Performance Indicator	**Information to be collected**
3 Pupil perception of computer usage in each subject area and overall.	Pupil Questionnaire Year Group .... (For use near the end of the term) (a) How often have you used a computer in each of your subjects? Put the correct 'score' alongside each subject you study. Put an X in the box if you do not take the subject. 0 = no use 1 = at least once this term 2 = at least once a month on average this term 3 = at least once per week on average this term

Information Source
(Where the information
can be obtained and
how to acquire it.)

Pupil questionnaire to
be administered by
form tutors.

Results to be collated
by senior managers.
(Analysis sheet
appended.)

Subjects	Score for using a computer
English	
Welsh*	
Maths	
Science	
Technology	
History	
Geography	
Modern Foreign Language e.g. French, German	
PE	

*For schools in Wales

(b) Taking all subjects together, how often have
you used a computer this term? Put the correct
'score' (0, 1, 2 or 3) in the box. [ ]

(c) If you wish, use the back of this sheet to say
what you most like and dislike about using
computers.

© Routledge 1992

Figure 3.5 Analysis sheet for IT3 questions a and b

IT ACROSS THE CURRICULUM

Performance Indicator: Pupil perception of computer usage in each subject
                                    area and overall

SUMMARY OF PUPIL DATA FOR YEAR GROUP   ....

DATE IT3 SHEETS COMPLETED   ....

Question (a)

SUBJECTS	COHORT TOTAL	NO USE (0)		AT LEAST ONCE A TERM (1)		AT LEAST ONCE A MONTH (2)		AT LEAST ONCE A WEEK (3)	
		No.	% of Cohort	No.	% of Cohort	No.	% of Cohort	No.	% of Cohort
English									
Welsh*									
Mathematics									
Science									
Technology									
History									
Geography									
Modern Language									
PE									

*For schools in Wales

Question (b)

Score	Tally	No.	%
0			
1			
2			
3			
	Total		

Figure 3.6 Information sources and data collection methods (p.i)

Information source	Method	Major advantages	Major disadvantages
People e.g. staff, pupils, parents, employers	Questionnaire	• Collects information from a large sample cost-effectively • Yields specific and comparative data • Allows respondents to remain anonymous	• Time-consuming to write and analyse • Questions can be misinterpreted by respondent • Responses may be superficial; in-depth questioning difficult • Questions may miss some important facets
	Interviews and conversations (one-to-one or group)	• Follows up responses, checks initial information • May reveal interviewees' real perceptions/attitudes • More flexible and friendly than paper exercise • Group situation may encourage individuals to speak more freely • Groups allow the views of more individuals to be collected	• Time-consuming to plan, administer, write up and analyse • The interviewer can influence the interviewee in a one-to-one situation • A group may be dominated by one or two individuals
Statistics, reports and other records of past events	Analysis of documentary/data base sources, including reported assessment of pupils' work	• Provides a record of events over a period of time • Provides a useful overview where data are readily available, and is a cost-effective source of specific and detailed information	• Records may be incomplete, inaccurate, or out of date • May be difficult to collect, collate or analyse data presented in an inappropriate form • Limited in applicability

Figure 3.6 Information sources and data collection methods (p.ii)

Information source	Method	Major advantages	Major disadvantages
	Analysis of planning documents	• May provide an indication of the state of development uninfluenced by the evaluator's presence/questionnaire • Gives rapid overview • Helps target aspects for in-depth evaluation and assists evaluator's understanding of the context	• Reality may not match rhetoric • Detail may be insufficient for evaluation purposes
Teaching/ learning situation	Observation	• Direct, 'first-hand' information • May reveal facts not anticipated by evaluator • May provide feedback from evaluator to teacher	• Observation may alter learning environment, inhibiting both staff and pupils • Observation and analysis are time-consuming • Risk of subjective judgements • Only provides a 'snapshot'
	Pupils' work	• Provides a longer-term view encompassing several weeks/months • Easily accessible with minimal disruption to normal practice	• Time-consuming to monitor a statistically valid sample • Application of objective evaluation criteria made difficult by the variability of the material

INFORMATION SOURCES AND DATA COLLECTION METHODS

For schools, information sources fall into three broad categories:

- people, including staff, pupils, parents, employers;
- statistics, reports and other records.
- the teaching and learning situation;

Since evaluation can be very time-consuming, it is best to consider carefully which information source will yield the relevant data with the minimum of disruption to normal practice. Data collection methods likewise need to be chosen with this basic requirement to the fore. Figure 3.6 lists the data collection methods most commonly used with these three information sources, and outlines their associated advantages and disadvantages. This list is not exhaustive, but indicates the sources and methods most readily used by schools.

When evaluation has been established within a school, and staff have developed a range of evaluation skills, all the methods outlined in Figure 3.6 can be used as appropriate. However, when getting started on evaluation, it may be advisable to avoid initially the use of observation and open-ended interviewing. Where a school is seeking to embed a systematic approach to evaluation in its practice, it should make the process acceptable to staff. The school should take the positive step of involving as many teachers as possible, and avoiding the negative aspect of collecting data in potentially threatening ways, for example, by direct observation of lessons at an early stage in embedding evaluation. Practical experience in evaluation is needed to develop the skills of designing effective instruments. This experience can be gained relatively quickly and over a wide range of issues by making use of questionnaires and analysis of documentary and data-base sources of information. Classroom observation and interviewing, for the purpose of recording conversations (one-to-one or in groups) both require additional skills beyond those needed for evaluation instrument design. We suggest that it is wise to ensure the instrument design is reasonably secure before embarking on situations that involve recording human interactions.

In making decisions about which methods or combination of methods to use, there are some additional practical considerations to be borne in mind. Broadly, these are concerned with sample selection, the personnel administering the data collection, and the timing of data collection.

Sample selection

When people are the source of information, a decision about how many of them to include in the survey has to be made. Except for short, simple questionnaires, it is rarely practicable to use the whole population (for example, the whole staff or all the pupils or all their parents). Exactly how many to sample will usually be determined by the amount of time which can be devoted to the evaluation, matched with the need to collect sufficient data from which justifiable conclusions can be drawn. As a rule of thumb, a survey should be used on at least one-third of the individuals in a given population or thirty people, whichever is the higher (Cohen and Manion, 1989: 104).

The selection of those to be included also needs to be considered. In a school situation, simple random sampling is rarely satisfactory because the total number of people involved is not large enough. Stratified random sampling will give results which are more likely to be valid for the targeted population as a whole. For example, stratification by ability and gender can often be achieved quite easily. Secondary schools usually set children for mathematics, hence mathematics teaching groups can be used as an indication of ability. To draw up a stratified random sample, the evaluator needs the mathematics group lists alphabetically but split into girls and boys. The selection of the third, sixth, ninth pupil, etc. from these lists provides a random sample, proportionately stratified by ability and gender – that is, the number sampled from each stratum is proportionate to the total number in that stratum in the whole cohort.

The factors to be taken into account may vary according to the nature of the evaluation focus. In general, the following will often apply for sampling pupils: gender, ability, ethnicity, language, teaching group, age (where survey spans more than one year group).

For convenience, a school may be tempted to choose one particular teaching group as the information source. In such a case, the individual circumstances affecting that group may severely limit the applicability of any inferences drawn from the data collected.

Personnel administering the data collection

Whatever sources of information are chosen, there is a need to decide on who will administer the collection. In most cases, a team approach will be adopted. This can have advantages in that it increases the extent of teacher involvement in the evaluation, allows the use of expertise appropriately, and it shares the workload. Further, it can allow collection of pupil data to occur during normal lessons and thereby minimise disruption to the school day. However, there is a serious risk that individuals will interpret evaluation instruments differently, and this can affect the validity of the data collected.

This can be minimised by providing a thorough briefing session for all staff involved, which includes opportunities for them to raise queries about the instrument. The first time an instrument is trialled, it is also valuable to meet briefly again after the data collection exercise to clear up whatever problems have arisen.

Timing the data collection

Some information needs to be collated only once yearly: numerical data relating to equipment or staffing levels; external examination results; and pupil destinations. Other data, particularly where curriculum development is involved, are best collected more frequently both to measure the extent of change and to aid the ongoing development, as highlighted in Chapter 2.

FRAMING EVALUATION QUESTIONS

The final step in completing the evaluation planning proforma (Figure 3.1) is to specify the information to be collected: in other words, to frame evaluation questions that are clear and unambiguous.

The process of completing the evaluation planning proforma helps staff to think through what precisely will show whether each specific objective is being met. Writing suitable questions is an acid test. It shows up whether the thinking has been woolly or rigorous, and forges the links between what may appear as rather theoretical objectives and the practical reality. It is crucial to keep in mind together the objective, the performance indicator(s), the information source(s) and the associated evaluation questions. Initially, the questions may be framed in a way which is technically naïve. Yet identifying what needs to be asked is the crux, and deciding how to ask it effectively is a matter of refinement.

The training described in Part II of this book is geared to help staff develop the skills required to identify what needs to be asked. They will also need some help in the framing of the evaluation questions and should be encouraged to experiment with a range of types. As initial guidance, the following examples may help to illustrate some possibilities.

Structured questions

These provide a framework within which the question must be answered. They have the advantage of being relatively easy to analyse and of ensuring that

Figure 3.7 Types of structured questions

1 Simple YES/NO type questions
2 Degree of agreement (scaling devices)
3 Categories
4 Item checklist or itemising
5 Scoring
6 Ranking
7 Grid or matrix
© Routledge 1992

Figure 3.8 Examples of structured questions (p.i)

1 Simple YES/NO type questions

These provide respondents with a very limited choice.

● **Example**

Do you find the work experience provided helpful in making a decision about your career?

☐ YES   ☐ NO

2 Degree of agreement (scaling devices)

Often a simple yes/no does not allow the respondent to indicate what s/he would like to state. A graded response can be more valuable.

● **Example**

In your opinion, was the work experience provided helpful in making decisions about your career? Note the 'degree of help' by placing an X on the scale below.

No Help			Limited Help	Some Help				Extremely Helpful
0	1	2	3	4	5	6	7	8	9	10

● **Example**

The work experience was worthwhile

Strongly Agree	Agree	Neutral	Disagree	Strongly Disagree
5	4	3	2	1

(Ring one number on the scale)

It is also possible to gain more detail by inviting extended comment:

I found the work experience was worthwhile/not worthwhile because

....

....

....

Figure 3.8 Examples of structured questions (p.ii)

---

3 Categories

Here a number of categories is offered from which the respondent ticks the most appropriate.

- **Example**

How many years teaching experience do you have?

Less than 2 years	
At least 2 years but less than 5 years	
At least 5 years but less than 10 years	
At least 10 years but less than 20 years	
20 years or more	

4 Item checklist or itemising

Checklists can be used to elicit responses to a number of possibilities or over a range of issues.

- **Example**

Where did you receive the advice/information that helped you decide on the course that you are following at the present moment?
(You may tick more than one box)

Careers teacher	
Other teachers	
Interview with careers officer	
School or college prospectus	
JIIG–CAL (Jobs Ideas and Information Generator – Computer Assisted Learning)	
Work experience	
Careers convention	
Parents or other relatives	
Friends	
Other – please specify	

Figure 3.8 Examples of structured questions (p.iii)

5 Scoring

This allows the respondent to make a comparative judgement.

- **Example**

To what extent did the following influence your choice on the course that you are following at present?

	Score	Score
Careers teacher		4 = almost entirely
Other teachers		3 = a great deal
Interview with careers officer		2 = some influence
School or college prospectus		1 = a little
JIIG–CAL (Jobs Ideas and Information Generator – Computer Assisted Learning		0 = not at all
Work experience		
Careers convention		
Parents or other relatives		
Friends		
Other – please specify		

6 Ranking

This requires the respondent to place various items in order of value or importance.

- **Example**

If you often stay away from school without permission, what are your reasons? Put your reasons in order of importance from 1 to 7, where 1 is the most important and 7 the least.

	Rank
I find the lessons boring	
My friends want me to go with them	
I have not done the homework set	
I have something better to do out of school	
I am afraid of some other pupils	
I am afraid of some teachers	
Something else – say what	

Figure 3.8 Examples of structured questions (p.iv)

---

7 Grid or matrix

These allow the recording of answers to two or more questions at the same time. They are often useful devices for collating information gathered from a number of sources.

- **Example**

What are the number of percentages of girls and boys following courses in one or more modern foreign languages in Year 10?

Pupils / Course	Girls		Boys		Total	
	No.	%	No.	%	No.	%
One GCSE						
Two or more GCSEs						
One non-GCSE course						
Two or more non-GCSE courses						
One GCSE and one non-GCSE course						
All modern foreign language courses						

respondents are provided with various categories which the questioner wishes them to consider. There is the risk that the evaluator may have missed some crucial issues. Further, respondents may find none of the categories offered is appropriate. These disadvantages can usually be overcome when the instrument is refined in the light of experience. Figure 3.7 lists various types of structured questions and Figure 3.8 provides examples of structured questions.

Unstructured questions

Such questions lead the respondent into considering a particular issue or topic but leave the form of response open ended. These have the advantage of allowing respondents the freedom to mention whatever they feel is appropriate and they are not restricted by the preconceptions of the evaluator. They are more valuable in an interview situation where the interviewer can probe more deeply to clarify the initial response. They are far less satisfactory in written questionnaires.

Unstructured questions can require:

- a factual answer, for example, 'What is the title of your post?'
- value judgements, for example, 'How are you involved in discussion prior to policy decisions being made?'

Often this second type of question will give rise to an extended answer which may be the source of much qualitative information. Unstructured questions can, however, leave a lot of issues unaddressed and they are usually much more difficult to analyse than structured questions.

ANALYSIS AND USE OF DATA

Analysis

When framing evaluation questions, it is always worth thinking about how to analyse the data that will result. Data that will be complex and time-consuming to handle may prove almost useless. In general, data which have been aggregated by someone else are certainly good news! For example, published GCSE results in aggregated form are much less troublesome than trying to analyse all the returns on individual pupils.

None the less, in many situations an analysis of raw data has to be undertaken. The literature on this, as with everything else we have discussed in this chapter, is vast. Clearly, the way the data should be collated and analysed must be determined by the objective being evaluated. We include in Figure 3.9 a few basic techniques to match the examples given in Figure 3.8.

Use and dissemination of the data

The final stage in this process is that of drawing inferences from the data and

Figure 3.9 Examples of analysis techniques (p.i)

Example 1 – YES/NO type

Use a simple tally chart to count the responses, for example:

涮 涮 |

It may be worthwhile to quote the final result as a percentage.

Examples 2 and 3 – Scaling devices + categories

Similarly, use a tally chart to total the number of each type of response, for example:

Degree of agreement	Scale	Tally	Frequency	Percentage
Strongly agree	5	| | |	3	
Agree	4	涮 |	6	
Neutral	3	涮 涮	10	
Disagree	2	涮 涮 |	11	
Strongly disagree	1		etc.	
		Total		

Example 4 – Itemising

Use a tally chart to pick out the most and least common responses. It might be worth putting the aggregated results in rank order or calculating the percentage of students who had used a particular advice/information source.

Figure 3.9 Examples of analysis techniques (p.ii)

Example 5 – Scoring

Use a tally chart to count the frequency of each response and then multiply the frequency by the 'score'.
For example, Advice/Information source is <u>Career teacher</u>.

Score	×4	×3	×2	×1	×0	Total
Frequency	1	5	29	12	3	50
Total Score	4	15	58	12	0	99

	Standardised Score	1.98

The standardised score can be calculated by dividing the total score in the shaded box by the number of responses. Here 99 ÷ 50 = 1.98. The standardised scores can then be compared for each advice/information source. Data collected on various occasions can also be compared in this way.

Example 6 – Ranking

Similar to Example 5. The average ranking can be calculated: divide the total in the shaded box by the number of respondents.

Example 7 – Grid or matrix

The information is usually already in collated form. However, if, for example, only numbers have been quoted, it may be necessary to calculate percentages.

making wider use of the results through dissemination. Both require careful handling.

Information collected in a self-evaluation exercise should not be treated as definitive. It can give some indication of the level of success or degree of progress. It may sound an alarm bell that some aspects of the curriculum or school life merit further attention. It should always be viewed in relation to other information, much of which will have been gleaned in the daily business of working in or with the school.

This leads on to a consideration of how the data should be used and disseminated within the school. The principles of evaluation, data dissemination and use should already have been established, and an ethics statement should have been agreed in advance. Decisions about how to use the specific information unearthed by the evaluation should be made in accordance with this general ethical statement. Each school will need to balance the degree of confidentiality to be maintained against the desire to use evaluation information as openly as possible. We suggest that the crucial questions are these.

- How can this information be used to promote development?
- Who needs this information and why?
- When do they need the information to make best use of it?
- What are the likely consequences of disseminating/withholding this information?

These and other issues raised in the present and the earlier chapters of Part I of this book need to be addressed in a practical context.

The training described in Part II aims to provide participants with the opportunity of learning the art of evaluation through practical experience.

Staff development and instrument design

Chapter 4

A training approach

When a school decides that there is need for internal or self-evaluation to aid planning and decision-making, the next step must involve equipping staff to operate a suitable evaluation system and developing evaluation instruments suited to the school's own priorities. The training approach outlined in this book aims to achieve both of these goals. Its main aims are:

- to engender positive attitudes among key personnel towards systematic evaluation;
- to provide these key personnel with the relevant knowledge and skills to set up and operate a limited exercise in school-based evaluation;
- to produce a starter bank of evaluation instruments for this limited exercise;
- to provide key personnel with structured opportunities to review the trial evaluation in preparation for embarking on a whole-school approach.

We have tried to provide enough detailed guidance to allow school managers or LEA trainers to operate this approach without they themselves having to go through the process first. The main prerequisite would be commitment to a planned and integrated evaluation system, one where the positive attitudes, as stated in the first aim, are already in place. Nevertheless, we recognise that first-hand experience of the process would be beneficial for training the trainers. Thus, for example, an LEA trainer could use this approach to develop senior managers in schools, for whom this book would be a major resource in training their own staff thereafter.

DESIGNING AN EFFECTIVE TRAINING PROGRAMME

There has been a great deal of research into the features of effective training programmes. A rough synthesis of their conclusions suggest that good courses have the following features:

- collaborative planning involving course leaders, LEA sponsors and former or prospective participants;
- a clear focus upon participants' current and future needs;

- careful preparatory briefing for participants several weeks ahead of the course, with opportunities for *pre-course work* where appropriate;
- a programme which is structured but has enough flexibility to allow for modifications in the light of monitoring and formative evaluation;
- a programme which is orientated towards *experience, practice and action*, and using as appropriate, methods like action learning, action research, performance feedback and *on-the-job assistance*;
- *'sandwich' timetable*, including course-based and job-based experiences to facilitate this approach;
- careful debriefing after the course and sustained support, ideally including on-the-job assistance where new skills are being implemented.

(Bolam 1987; authors' italics)

The training model which we have developed incorporates these elements.

THE TRAINING MODEL

Figure 4.1 illustrates the model diagrammatically.

Prerequisites

The effectiveness of the model rests initially on four main requirements:

- the existence of specific curriculum development plans from which areas for evaluation will be selected;
- commitment from the participating schools to trialling systematic evaluation as an integral feature of the management cycle;
- the operation of suitable procedures for the identification of training needs, so that the staff who are to receive the training acknowledge this as a professional development need for them;
- a course leader with a good understanding of the issues and experience in training teachers.

Pre-briefing

The purpose of the pre-briefing is to give an overview of the whole training programme and to agree on the pre-course work which participants will undertake before Conference 1.

Pre-course work

To make best use of the conference time, participants should ensure that they are thoroughly familiar with their school development plan and that they have consulted with other members of staff and identified priority areas for evaluation.

Figure 4.1 'King-burger' training programme including course-based and job-based experience

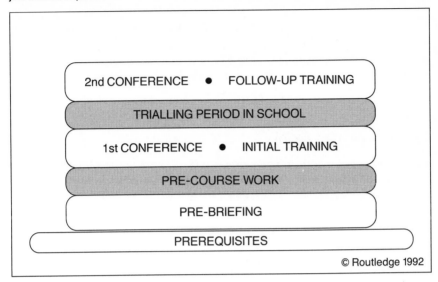

Conference 1 – initial training

The scope of the initial training is to give key personnel:

- an appreciation of the need for systematic evaluation as an integral part of management;
- an understanding of some of the basic principles of evaluation with exemplars provided for illustration;
- the opportunity to devise evaluation instruments to meet their own chosen curricular priorities, and to discuss the operational requirements of trialling these instruments.

Trialling period in school

During this period, course participants will have the chance to set up and run a limited trial evaluation, using the instruments produced during Conference 1. This should include the involvement of other staff in using the instruments and collating comments on the trial, to feed into Conference 2.

Course participants can get on-the-job assistance by liaising with others involved in a similar exercise, since discussing both progress and problems should be mutually supportive.

Conference 2 – follow-up training

The scope of the follow-up training is:

- to enhance understanding of data collection methods, data analysis, interpretation and dissemination, including the ethics of evaluation;
- to refine the evaluation instruments in the light of trialling;
- to consider how to move forward to a whole-school approach.

Participants' feedback of their experiences is a pivotal feature in this conference.

BENEFITS OF THIS MODEL

The model aims to set the training firmly in the context of the school's perceived priorities and not in a contrived situation. In effect, participants are undertaking action research which is directly relevant to their work and concerns.

The 'king-burger' model is important on three counts. First, by ensuring that the theory of the training is put into immediate practice, it helps ensure that the knowledge and skills acquired during the first conference are reinforced through continuing practical experience. Second, it provides an experiential basis on which to build a deeper level of understanding during the second conference. Third, its structure allows the trainers to use part of Conference 2 to evaluate participants' perceptions of the training up to that point. This would include participants' experience of how well the training had equipped them to cope during the trialling period. It could be undertaken through the familiar end-of-conference written questionnaire coupled perhaps with observation data collected during the working sessions of Conference 2.

The material outcomes, namely the evaluation instruments, are tangible products which both provide a focus for participants' efforts and are useful in themselves when the training is over.

TIME-SCALE

Figure 4.2 illustrates a possible time-scale for this training process which attempts to marry the training with the management cycle. It is designed so that:

- curriculum development plans are finalised prior to the pre-briefing;
- start of trialling corresponds with the start of the school year, so that evaluation data can be collected at suitable times and help inform future planning;
- Conference 2 occurs early enough to allow for a whole-school approach to be started in the following September.

This timing was devised for training one deputy headteacher from each of a cluster or consortium of schools. For in-school training, the timing would need to be modified so as to make appropriate use of closure days for staff development and to avoid the peak periods of pupil assessment. The following pattern, modifying the programmes given later in this chapter could be adopted.

Figure 4.2 Time-scale for the training process

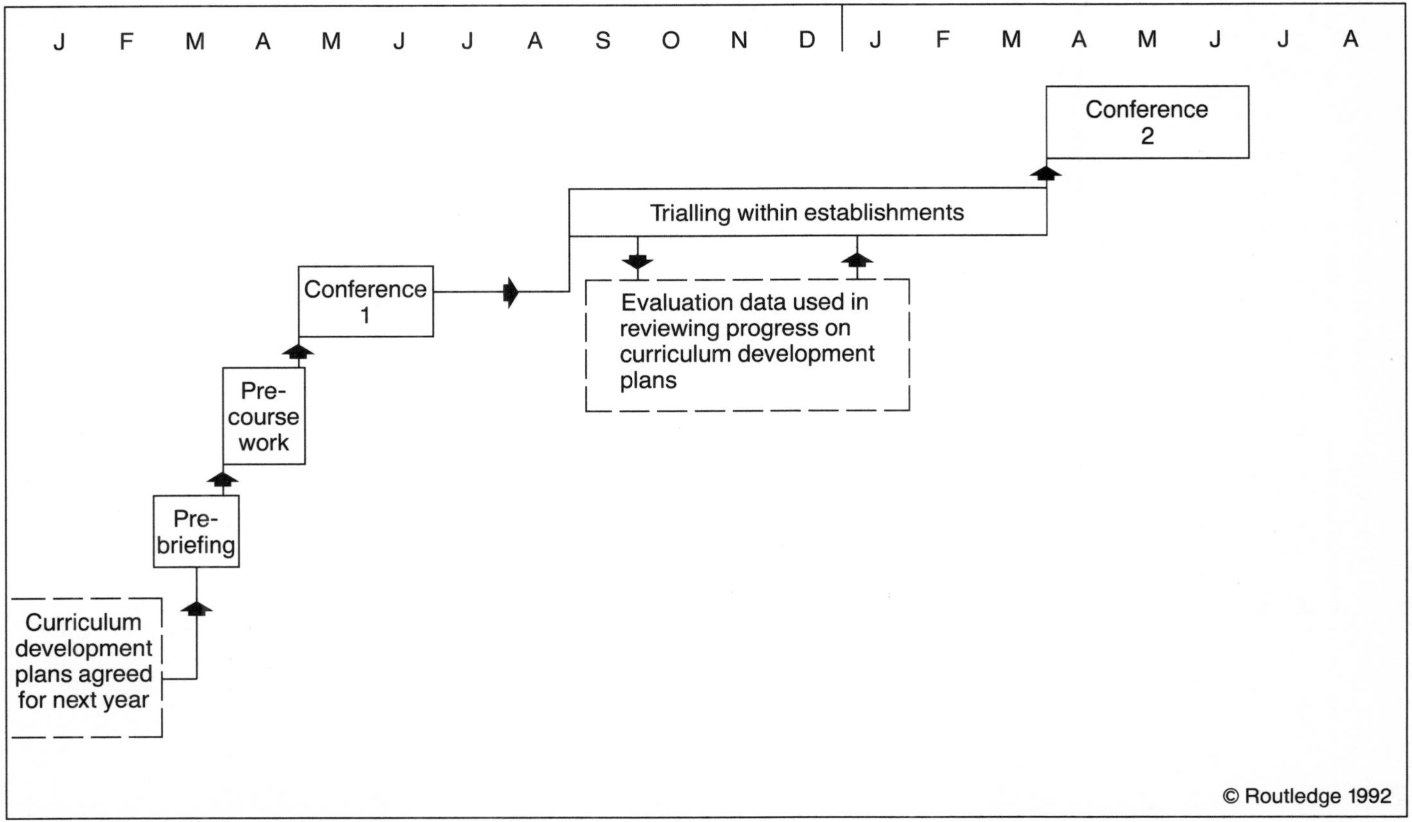

© Routledge 1992

Pre-briefing   To be undertaken in a staff meeting.

Pre-course work   To be undertaken through formal and informal discussions
                     between members of curricular/year teams.

Conference 1   Programme for Day 1 to be run during an INSET closure day;
                     programme for Day 2 to be undertaken during curricular/year
                     team meetings, with a full staff meeting for the issues raised in
                     the plenary.

Trialling   Best spread over two terms, but could be reduced if necessary.

Conference 2   Could be restructured to use the morning programme during
                     half a closure day; afternoon programme would be under-
                     taken during curricular/year team meetings with a staff meet-
                     ing to replace the final plenary.

Chapter 5

The training process – first phase

In both this chapter and the next, for each of the course-based elements in the training process we use the following symbols:

- objectives

- a programme

- tasks for workshop

All the training materials provided are suitable for use as handouts. In addition, we give supplementary guidance. This includes reference to appropriate materials and overhead projector transparencies from other chapters of this book which can be used as the basis for inputs.

For the job-based elements, we provide objectives for use as handouts together with supplementary notes for the trainer.

PRE-BRIEFING

(Suggested timing: February/March, 1–2 hour meeting)
The course leader can make use of the material in Chapter 4 for the input describing the training programme. Figures 4.1 and 4.2 are suitable as overhead projector transparencies.

PRE-BRIEFING: **objectives**

1   To provide participants with an overview of the King-burger training programme.

2   To agree with participants the preparation they need to undertake prior to the course to include:

(i) identifying the priority development areas and associated specific objectives for evaluation;

(ii) identifying those colleagues who will be involved in the proposed evaluation exercise and how best to win their support.

© Routledge 1992

PRE-BRIEFING: **programme**

INPUT: Description of the training programme

WORKSHOP: Putting the training in context

PLENARY: Agreeing the pre-conference preparations

© Routledge 1992

The following questions will need to be answered in the workshop.

PRE-BRIEFING: **tasks for workshop**

1   What areas should have priority for evaluation next year?

2   Are there clear agreed objectives for development in these areas? If not, what needs to be done, by whom and when?

3   Who will need to be involved with you if you undertake evaluation in these areas? How will you negotiate their roles with them? By when?

4   Is the proposed timing of the training (including the trialling) acceptable? If there are problems, how can they be overcome?

© Routledge 1992

Where the training is school based, there is a need to reach consensus on determining the priority areas for evaluation in order to limit the scope of the evaluation exercise.

Where senior managers of a number of schools are being trained together, it helps greatly if schools can agree to some measure of commonality so that the work of writing evaluation instruments can be shared and so that the trialling provides feedback from more than one source.

Where LEA personnel are being trained, the workshop questions must be set in the context of how to reach agreement with the schools in which the advisers hope to undertake the trialling.

The function of the plenary is to clarify:

- what precisely has been agreed;
- what pre-course work is necessary prior to Conference 1.

PRE-COURSE WORK

(Suggested timing: March–May)

PRE-COURSE WORK: **objectives**	
1 To become thoroughly informed about the school development plan. 2 To agree with colleagues on three or four priority areas for evaluation. 3 To enlist the support of key personnel for the trialling exercise. <div align="right">© Routledge 1992</div>	

Staff working in school need to familiarise themselves with the school's development plan, including areas which normally lie outside their sphere of interest. Agreement with colleagues on three or four priority areas can be reached more readily when there is a shared understanding of what the school as a whole hopes to achieve. This consultation process can itself help to win over colleagues to be involved in the trialling.

For LEA personnel, the pattern is entirely parallel, although they have to overcome more resistance because they may be viewed as outsiders. Additional time to work with the schools may be needed and staff may need to be convinced that the proposed trialling has advantages for them.

The timing for the first main training day will depend on how much more spade-work remains to be done after the pre-briefing, in agreeing priority areas and in liaising with other colleagues. It should not be more than a month or two!

CONFERENCE 1: INITIAL TRAINING

(Suggested timing: May/June, two-day conference)

CONFERENCE 1: **objectives**

---

1 To present and discuss the rationale of evaluation.

2 To present and discuss the place of evaluation within the management cycle.

3 To give experience of devising performance indicators linked to specific objectives.

4 To give experience of designing evaluation instruments for measurement of those PIs.

5 To discuss the operational aspects of using the evaluation instruments devised.

6. To agree on a limited trial to be undertaken within establishments.

© Routledge 1992

CONFERENCE 1: **programme for Day 1**	

	DAY 1 — MORNING (Objectives 1, 2, 3)
INPUT A	• Evaluation: its rationale and place within the management cycle. • Performance Indicators: their link with specific objectives and desired outcomes.
BRIEFING	Workshop 1: Devising performance indicators to measure specific objectives. Workshop 2: Checking suitability for purpose.
WORKSHOP 1	Each group to work on selected curricular area(s).
WORKSHOP 2	Groups will work in pairs: each group will review the PIs produced by its partner group, comment on their suitability for purpose and feed back to author group; paired groups to agree on improved PIs for use in the next workshop.
	AFTERNOON (Objective 4)
INPUT B	Designing evaluation instruments.
BRIEFING	Workshop 3: Completing evaluation planning proformas.
WORKSHOP 3	Each group to complete a first draft of an evaluation planning instrument with its associated data collection detailed.
PLENARY	Progress to date: summary of lessons learnt. Course leader to receive comments from participants and provide summative overview.

© Routledge 1992

CONFERENCE 1: **programme for Day 2**

	DAY 2 — MORNING (Objectives 4, 5)
INTRODUCTION AND BRIEFING	Workshop 4: Checking the evaluation questions' suitability for purpose.
WORKSHOP 4	Group will work in pairs; each group will review the draft produced by its partner group, comment on its suitability for purpose and feed back to the author group; paired groups to agree on improved draft.
INPUT AND BRIEFING	Workshop 5: Operational aspects of evaluation.
	AFTERNOON (Objectives 5, 6)
WORKSHOP 5	Each group to discuss the operational aspects of evaluation in relation to at least two selected evaluation instruments produced in Workshops 3 and 4 for feed back to a plenary session.
PLENARY	Feedback on the operational aspects of using the evaluation instruments produced in this conference.
	Agreement on what is to be trialled within establishments.
	Arrangements for support during trialling.

Material from Chapters 1 and 2 can be used for input A, with overhead projector transparencies selected from the various figures so as to build on the existing knowledge and experience of participants.

An outline of the task in Workshop 1 is given below (a suitable proforma for this purpose was given in Figure 3.1).

CONFERENCE 1: **tasks for Workshop 1**

Devising PIs to measure specific objectives

Complete the sections relating to aims, objectives and PIs on the proformas provided for each of the curricular areas allocated to your group.

If the objectives suggested are not sufficiently specific, you may need to recast them before fixing your PIs. It may be helpful to consider how you would recognise that the desired outcome for each objective has been reached.

© Routledge 1992

This workshop assumes that priority areas for evaluation will already have been agreed in principle at the pre-briefing meeting. However, if after the pre-course work the participants return with widely differing priorities, there will be need to provide opportunity for some further negotiations. This should determine, as quickly as possible, whether to work on the majority interest(s) only or whether to accommodate the diverse views but with a reduction in mutual support during both the conference sessions and the trialling period.

Participants wishing to focus on the same curricular area should work together, first agreeing on common aims and objectives, and then moving on to suggest suitable performance indicators. They should complete the relevant parts of the proforma provided to pass on to their pair group in Workshop 2. Because groups work at different rates, it can be useful to have a coffee break between Workshops 1 and 2. This allows the slower groups additional time to finish the tasks, ready for Workshop 2.

A checklist approach to testing performance indicators' fitness for purpose is provided in the tasks for Workshop 2. In this session, groups are paired. Each group works for about one-third of the available time on its pair group's performance indicators. The two groups then combine, share findings and revise their performance indicators in the light of discussion. The chairperson's role is crucial here: the task needs to be finished (by lunch!). Discussion must be kept focused and any tendency to agonise over minor issues should be avoided. This is in itself an important part of the training since school life is much too full to allow such tasks unlimited amounts of time and effort.

CONFERENCE 1: **tasks for Workshop 2**

Checking the suitability of PIs to the purposes

(a) Consider the PIs provided by your pair group, and determine the extent to which each PI is suited to the purposes by answering at least the following questions:

1   Does the PI provide a measure of the objective?
    If not, it will have to be rewritten.
2   Who benefits from the information which the PI provides?
    The answers here are crucial in determining whether it is worth going on to design the data collection for this PI.
3   Is the PI directly measurable?
    If how to obtain the measure is not immediately obvious, the author group will need to provide further information. Indeed it may be necessary to recast the PI.
4   Is the PI easy to measure?
    If not, the author group will have to consider whether the effort involved in collecting the information is likely to be justified in terms of the benefits of having access to the data.
5   Is the PI unambiguous and is the language used easy to understand?
    If not, the authors will need both to try simplifying the language and to take particular care in framing the evaluation questions associated with the PI.
6   Are any additional PIs needed to give an improved measure of the objective?
    If so, the reader group should write down their suggested additions.
7   Are there any other comments you wish to make?

(b) Join with your pair group and feed back your responses. If time allows, work together to produce an improved set of PIs for your allotted curricular areas.

It is essential that you complete the task since the PIs you produce here will form the basis for this afternoon's session.

© Routledge 1992

Material from Chapter 3 can be used for input B on designing evaluation instruments. The tasks for Workshop 3 are outlined on page 63. Writing evaluation instruments for the first time can be slow. The guidance given in Chapter 1 under the subheading 'Constraints' may be worth rehearsing as part of the briefing. As with the morning session, the chairperson's role is crucial to keep the momentum going. A first draft – no matter how imperfect – is the goal. It helps morale to finish the job.

The plenary session at the end of the day gives participants a chance to air their views. It also helps morale to realise that other groups were struggling just as hard. The course leader can use this opportunity to draw Day 1 to a close, pointing out just how much everyone has achieved and summarising some of the main lessons learnt.

Day 2 begins by welcoming participants back and briefing them for Workshop 4 which is outlined on pages 64 and 65. As in Workshop 2, groups are paired with the aim of refining the evaluation questions. Again, maintaining momentum to complete the task requires determination. Completion is important to ensure that the instruments to be trialled have been fully agreed by the participants. If time runs out, the course organiser can complete the job, perhaps with the help of a small group of fellow enthusiasts. But those trialling the instruments will be far less conversant with what the instruments seek to achieve, and the trialling may therefore be less effective. Worse, the participants may object to some of the methods of data collection suggested.

Finally, Workshop 5 is much better run with the actual instruments which participants will be trialling than with prepared exemplars. It is much more helpful to discuss the issues you are going to face than to speculate on theoretical possibilities.

CONFERENCE 1: **tasks for Workshop 3**

Completing evaluation planning proforma

Complete the evaluation instrument planning proforma for your chosen curricular area:

1 by indicating the method by which data will be collected and who will be responsible;

2 by providing written details of the evaluation questions.

These may take the form of:

- a written questionnaire to be completed by staff and/or pupils;
- a questionnaire to be completed during a structured one-to-one interview;
- information to be gleaned from documentary/database sources.

If none of these is applicable, you may need to consider:

- a checklist to be used in an open-ended interview situation or in classroom observation.

Please discuss the use of observation or open-ended interview with the course leader before proceeding.

Remember to try and make your evaluation instrument as simple, unambiguous and time-efficient as possible. And always think: who needs to know this and why? Finally, you may find that the PI or even the objective needs refining as you get down to the detailed list of questions.

CONFERENCE 1: **tasks for Workshop 4**

Checking the evaluation questions' suitability

(a) You will be provided with your pair group's completed evaluation planning proforma and associated questions. The task of analysing them follows on from the analysis you undertook on the PIs in Workshop 2. Determine the extent to which the questions provided are suited to the purpose by answering at least the following:

1 Do the questions measure performance as defined by the PI?
   If not, they will have to be rewritten.
2 Are all the questions relevant? Who needs the information they supply and why?
   It is very tempting to ask more than is necessary when measuring any particular PI. Fewer requests for information are always welcome — especially by those who have to collect the data.
3 Are the questions unambiguous?
   If not, the data collected will not be reliable.
4 Will the questions elicit meaningful responses?
   If not, the data will be worthless.
5 Will collecting this information benefit the establishment sufficiently to justify the work involved?
   If not, is there an alternative source of information which does not involve the school in more work, or do we need an alternative way of measuring the extent to which the objective has been achieved?
6 Are the questions presented in a user-friendly way?
   If not, how could you improve/simplify the form and/or language?
7 Does the format display the information in a way that makes analysis straightforward?
   If not, it might be worth designing a supplementary analysis sheet to collate results.
8 Are the questions applicable to a range of establishments?
   *If they are very specific to the way in which the curriculum is organised in particular establishments, they will have limited use.**
9 Are there any other comments you wish to make?

(b) Join with your pair group and feed back your responses. If time allows, work together to produce a revised version of the evaluation planning proforma and associated questions. Alternatively, you may need to subdivide to finish the task. It is important to complete the task since the materials you produce will be needed for Workshop 5.

© Routledge 1992

*This question is important even where school-based training is involved, since instruments produced in one school could be shared with others in the local cluster or consortium. Even if a school produced instruments for internal use only, the underlying principle could still apply. For example, if the infant teacher in a primary school devised an instrument to evaluate the extent of parental involvement in their reading scheme, they should aim to make it applicable to key stage 2 as well as key stage 1. Likewise, if the scientists in secondary schools were concerned to evaluate the delivery of a particular cross-curricular competence, their evaluation instrument could be devised so as to be useful, not just in science teaching but throughout the school.

Input C, prior to Workshop 5, is not intended to be a long discourse on data collection and analysis. At this stage, some priorities should be selected from the issues raised in Chapter 3. The tasks for this workshop are provided on page 66. If participants completed Workshops 3 and 4, their results can be used for Workshop 5, as noted earlier. If not, other examples such as those provided in Chapter 3 of this book may be used.

At this stage in the training, participants' awareness should be raised in relation to the issues outlined in the workshop. A more structured attempt to address these issues will be undertaken in Conference 2, following practical trialling.

The plenary session at the end of this second day should be used, as indicated in the programme, for three purposes:

- to draw together any conclusions on the use of the evaluation instruments produced over the two-day conference;
- to clarify and agree which instruments are to be trialled and by whom;
- to outline the support available during the trialling period.

This support is best given by a pairing approach. The pairs may be formed on a social or geographical basis, or on grounds of similar situations (for example, where the same instrument is being trialled). Pairs should be encouraged to keep in regular contact, to discuss the operation of the evaluation exercise, and to share ideas and problems. This is particularly important where the course participants are not all members of one establishment.

A summary of the various prerequisites for successful trialling together with the desired outcomes of the exercise are illustrated in Figure 5.1. This figure provides an overview which links Conferences 1 and 2 through the trialling period.

CONFERENCE 1: **tasks for Workshop 5**

You are provided with examples of two completed evaluation planning proformas produced in previous workshop sessions. Try to provide general answers to the following questions from noting the issues raised by these evaluation instruments. You will be asked to feed back your responses in the plenary session.

1 How and when should the data be collected? Will it be necessary to use sampling techniques?

2 Which members of staff will be involved in the evaluation trialling? What needs to be done to enlist their support and co-ordinate the data collection?

3 How should the results be analysed? Is there a need for any additional guidelines to assist this analysis?

4 What factors should be taken into account in interpreting the data collected?

5 Who should be provided with the data? For what purposes do they need it, and when? In what form should the results be presented to them? What are the confidentiality parameters which need to be agreed?

6 What needs to be done to give the evaluation exercise a fair trial and to allow the staff and students involved to express their views about the evaluation instruments?

Figure 5.1 Trialling period

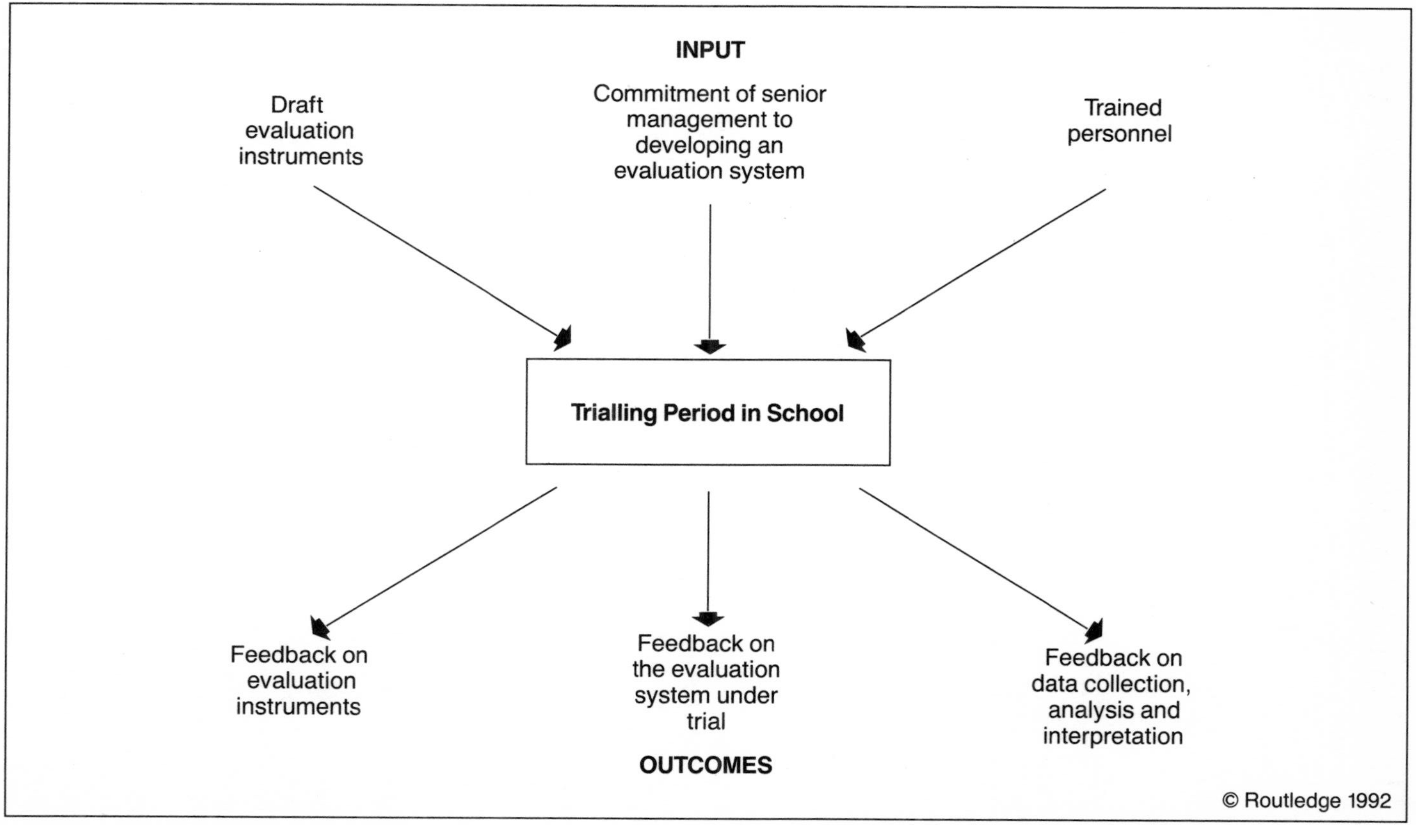

INPUT

Trained personnel

Commitment of senior management to developing an evaluation system

Draft evaluation instruments

Trialling Period in School

Feedback on data collection, analysis and interpretation

Feedback on the evaluation system under trial

OUTCOMES

Feedback on evaluation instruments

© Routledge 1992

Chapter 6

The training process – second phase

TRIALLING PERIOD IN SCHOOLS

(Suggested timing: September–May)

For the trialling to have any kind of chance, it is essential that the schools involved are committed to systematic evaluation. Although the training can be successful in fostering positive attitudes, even for participants who are un-committed, it will fail if those attitudes cannot be further developed through practical experience in school.

The trialling period is beneficial for each of the following:

- staff development, since it allows participants to make practical use of the knowledge and skills developed during the first conference; it also provides an experiential basis on which to build deeper insights during Conference 2;
- evaluation instrument design, since it allows the draft designs to be tested in practice under various circumstances;
- school development, since it provides an opportunity for small-scale pilot of an evaluation system.

Specific objectives for the trial are given below. As indicated in Figure 4.2, the evaluation should be made to fit within the management cycle of the establishment. Therefore nearly a full academic year is ideally allocated for the trial, although this can be reduced if necessary.

It can be all too easy for an evaluation system to be perceived as being not only intrusive but also causing already overburdened teachers yet more work. Some preparatory work with certain key members of staff will already have taken place after the pre-briefing meeting. It is now essential that these staff be fully involved in the planning stages of how to undertake the evaluation exercise within their school, and that the whole staff be consulted about the proposed trial.

The parameters of confidentiality should be made explicit, for example, through drafting an agreed ethics statement (see final section of Chapter 2). Some staff may also be involved in data collection and therefore it is important to clarify exactly what information is to be collected, also how, by whom and when. Particular care should be paid to any data collection involving students, since the responses given depend significantly on the way in which questions are posed. A

TRIALLING PERIOD: **objectives**

1 To set up and run a system within schools which will allow fair trialling of the draft evaluation instruments.

2 To involve all the relevant staff in:

- setting realistic targets against which to monitor progress;
- implementing the monitoring;
- making value judgements in the light of the information collected;
- using the results of the evaluation to inform forward planning.

3 To collect and collate comments from all the relevant parties (staff and students) in respect of the trialling, and to suggest ways of improving the evaluation.

© Routledge 1992

case study describing how one school dealt with these issues is provided in Chapter 7.

As indicated earlier, course participants should support one another during the trial. Discussion of the various sensitivities which arise as staff and students become involved in the evaluation exercise can be valuable.

Finally, the individual co-ordinating the evaluation exercise within school needs to plan how to gather feedback on the trialling. Staff should be provided with the opportunity to make constructive criticism and suggestions for improvement of any aspect of the evaluation.

CONFERENCE 2: FOLLOW-UP TRAINING

(Suggested timing: May/June, one-day conference)

CONFERENCE 2: **objectives**

1 To discuss the practicalities of data collection.

2 To identify various factors which must be taken into account in data analysis and interpretation.

3 To discuss the use and presentation of evaluation findings to a variety of interest groups.

4 To undertake the work necessary to refine the trialled evaluation instruments in the light of experience and further reflection.

5 To consider how to take the work forward so as to move to a whole-school approach.

© Routledge 1992

CONFERENCE 2: **programme**

	MORNING (Objectives 1, 2, 3)
INTRODUCTION	Brief overview of progress to date. Objectives of this conference.
INPUT	Lessons learnt from the trial.
BRIEFING	Workshop 1: data collection.
WORKSHOP 1	Each group to list its recommendations for collecting data from staff and students with reference to the evaluation instruments under consideration.
BRIEFING	Workshop 2: analysis, interpretation and use of data.
WORKSHOP 2	Each group to make recommendations on the above in respect of the evaluation instruments under consideration.
PLENARY A	General conclusions. Course leader to receive feedback from the groups and summarise main recommendations.
	AFTERNOON (Objectives 4 and 5)
BRIEFING	Workshop 3: revision of evaluation instruments.
WORKSHOP 3	Each group to edit and improve the evaluation instrument it produced during Conference 1 in the light of the trialling.
PLENARY B	The way forward.

© Routledge 1992

The introduction may start by looking again at Figure 5.1 as a reminder to participants of how the conference hopes to build on the outcomes of the trialling. The objectives outline the specific targets for the day.

The function of the input is to stimulate discussion for Workshops 1 and 2. It can take various forms, for example:

- one participant providing a case study of his/her experiences;
- three or four participants setting the scene, each describing a specific issue which arose during the trialling;
- the course organiser giving an overview from feedback obtained in advance from participants.

Workshop 1 focuses on issues arising from data collection involving staff and students. Each group should consider a set of evaluation instruments which has been trialled by at least some of the group members – ideally the whole group.

CONFERENCE 2: **tasks for Workshop 1**

Collecting data from staff and students

With reference to the evaluation instruments you have been asked to consider, make recommendations for each of the following. You may be asked to feed back your findings in the plenary session.

1 *Sample size*
   Consider the factors schools should take into account when deciding whether to use the whole cohort, a representative sample, or a random sample.

   If for pragmatic reasons a school chooses to use a particular teaching group as the sample, what are the possible implications that need to be borne in mind?

2 *Administering the data collection*
   Consider the implications of using either a single member of staff or a team of teachers to collect data from pupils or staff. The following points need to be borne in mind:

   • consistency of interpretation of the evaluation document;
   • the degree of disruption to normal practice;
   • the workload on individuals.

3 *Timing of data collection*
   Indicate the types of data collection that are best done more than once yearly and those where a single collection is sufficient.

© Routledge 1992

Workshop 2 is concerned with the analysis, interpretation and use of data. Group members should continue with the instruments they discussed in Workshop 1. In the morning plenary session, the course leader will need to structure the feedback to categorise the various points raised. The aim is to summarise findings in order both to help refine the instruments under consideration and also to give guidance for developing and using other instruments in the future.

Workshop 3 gives participants the opportunity of refining the evaluation instruments they produced in the first conference. The function of the final plenary session is to identify ways of moving forward to a whole-school approach. It can be run as a brainstorming session to involve participants. The course organiser will need to encourage participants to suggest various stages in developing a whole-school approach to evaluation.

The list given in Figure 6.1 indicates some possible stages. During this session it should become clear that the long-term goal is a fully integrated evaluation system, but there are smaller steps which can be taken to help achieve the grand plan. Further discussion of these issues is provided in Chapter 8.

CONFERENCE 2: **tasks for Workshop 2**

Data analysis, interpretation and use

With reference to the evaluation instruments you may have been asked to consider, make recommendations for each of the following, which you will be asked to feed back in the plenary session.

1 *Data analysis*
Did the trial materials facilitate analysis? If not, how should they be amended? You may wish to consider:

- how to collate and/or group the data;
- whether to score various responses;
- whether to convert raw numbers into percentages;
- whether to calculate average or modal (most frequent) responses.

2 *Interpretation of data*
What factors should be taken into account in interpreting data? You may wish to consider:

- the extent to which the data provide firm evidence for reaching a definite conclusion;
- the extent to which the apparent findings are borne out by information from other sources;
- the differences between data relating to staff or student perceptions/opinions and data of a more factual kind.

3 *Use and dissemination of data*
List the various interest groups who would benefit from having access to these data. By considering what use each group should make of information, suggest how best to present the relevant information to each group.

© Routledge 1992

CONFERENCE 2: **tasks for Workshop 3**

Revision of the evaluation instruments

In the light of this morning's discussions and using the comments you have received from staff and pupils involved in trialling, reconsider and, where necessary, improve the evaluation instrument you wrote in the last conference. Make the final document as user-friendly, unambiguous and generally applicable as possible.

© Routledge 1992

Figure 6.1 Possible stages in moving to a whole-school approach

ACTION	REASON FOR USE
Use improved version of evaluation instrument already trialled	(a) To follow progress of the same cohort of pupils over two years (b) To evaluate the effectiveness of the school's provision by comparing results from two successive cohorts
Use different instruments (produced and trialled by others)	(a) To extend the scope of the evaluation (b) To involve a wider range of staff
Set up a working party to draft a whole-school policy	(a) To integrate evaluation with other aspects of school's work (b) To involve all key personnel in agreeing the whole-school policy
Train other staff and simultaneously produce further instruments	(a) To equip staff with the skills and knowledge they need to implement whole-school policy (b) To design evaluation instruments which meet the school's priorities
Consider how information gathered through appraising staff and monitoring the use of material resources can be fed into the curriculum evaluation process	To operate an integrated management information system encompassing: ● the curriculum ● staff appraisal ● use of resources © Routledge 1992

It is also possible that participants may discuss the value of using the 'king-burger' training approach as an effective model for addressing other staff development needs. While the course organiser will not wish to constrain discussion, it is important to ensure that the focus is firmly on how to move forward with regards to evaluation in schools.

Part III

The way forward

Chapter 7

Embedding systematic evaluation

The training outlined in Part II ends by encouraging course participants to consider what the next steps should be. Where this training involves senior managers from several schools, each of these schools will need to decide how to move forward from the limited trial.

If the training and trialling are to be of any lasting value, the evaluation process must be institutionalised, that is, become a normal part of the establishment's practice.

The next logical step is to formulate a policy from which to derive specific objectives and targets for development, together with strategies for reaching those targets. However, at this early stage in getting started on evaluation, any policy is likely to be an interim statement which will be refined, extended and improved in the light of experience. It is important to have a vision, albeit somewhat blurred, of where the school is going, in order to share that vision with others.

The experience of one school in its early attempts to embed self-evaluation in its normal practice is outlined below.

CASE STUDY OF A SECONDARY SCHOOL

Dan yr Olwg (pseudonym) is a medium-sized, 11–18, naturally bilingual comprehensive school set in a small market town in rural Wales.

The school has a typical pyramidal management structure. The headteacher is supported by three deputies. Middle managers hold departmental/faculty/cross-curricular/pastoral areas of responsibility. The school comments:

> Regular staff, panel and committee meetings aim to obtain a consensus on all important issues. Information is regularly fed back to all staff and this is seen as an important issue as the school moves ever further towards a faculty and cross-curricular approach to teaching. The need for the evaluation of initiatives, cross-curricular co-operation and a planned programme of staff development have all been discussed by the appropriate body of staff and a consensus view agreed upon.

Figure 7.1 Trialling a structured, whole-school approach to evaluation

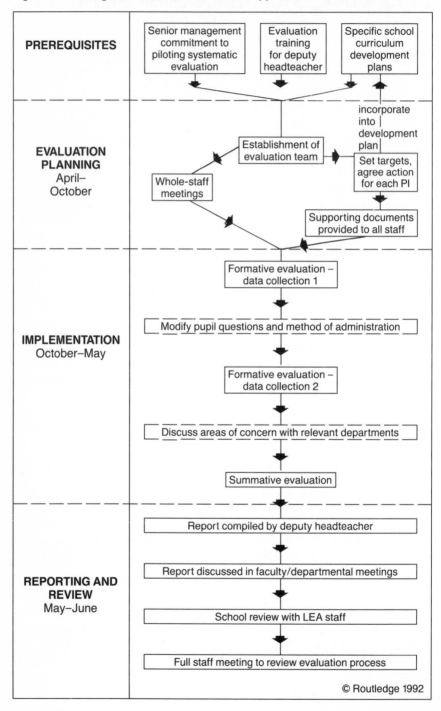

© Routledge 1992

One of Dan yr Olwg's deputy headteachers was trained in evaluation using an approach similar to that described in Part II. During the academic year 1990/91, Dan yr Olwg piloted a structured, whole-school approach to evaluation. The steps the school took are described in detail below and summarised diagrammatically in Figure 7.1.

Evaluation planning

As a result of the evaluation training, several schools working in consortia had produced evaluation instruments for a number of priority curricular issues. During autumn 1990, the consortium of which Dan yr Olwg was a member agreed on two priority curricular issues for evaluation in all the consortium schools, namely *information technology across the curriculum* and *special educational needs*. Dan yr Olwg also chose to evaluate two further issues, namely *records of achievement* and *bilingualism*. All four issues were important elements in its school development plan for 1990/91.

The majority of the evaluation instruments to be used had been produced and trialled elsewhere, although the deputy headteacher co-ordinating the evaluation work in Dan yr Olwg had been a member of the group which produced the instruments for evaluating bilingualism.

It was crucial to win over staff to the evaluation trial, particularly since they had not been involved in devising the instruments being used. The school used a combination of strategies:

- formation of an evaluation team;
- full staff meetings;
- supporting documentation provided to all staff.

The evaluation team

The senior management of Dan yr Olwg wished to adopt a team approach to evaluation involving key personnel. The team consisted of:

- a deputy headteacher to co-ordinate the work;
- the co-ordinators responsible for the four priority issues being evaluated;
- the head of middle school (since the evaluation was targeted on Year 10);
- the three Year 10 form tutors.

The four co-ordinators were provided with copies of the evaluation instruments. They were asked to consider the performance indicators and evaluation questions relating to their area of responsibility in order to:

- set realistic targets for the next academic year (1990/91);
- suggest what action was necessary to meet those targets and by whom;
- indicate by when this action should be taken.

They talked over their ideas with the co-ordinating deputy headteacher. Some revisions were agreed, particularly where the targets suggested were too ambitious. The targets were then discussed with the headteacher, and the agreed final version incorporated as part of the school's development plan.

The members of the evaluation team were also involved in planning and implementing the data collection. They considered the evaluation instruments in detail, and how the evaluation exercise would affect them as individuals. Their discussion included:

- the nature of the evaluation;
- the ways data would be collected;
- who would be involved in collecting data;
- the timing of data collection;
- the analysis of the data;
- the form of the final report;
- the dissemination strategy to the whole staff;
- action to follow up the evaluation.

The school comments: 'This was a key meeting to allay fears and any opposition felt about the school embracing evaluation as part of normal educational practice for the first time.'

The co-ordinating deputy headteacher was ultimately responsible for leading the team, for collating the information collected and for compiling an evaluation report.

Full staff meetings

In addition to evaluation team meetings, a meeting of the whole staff was used to introduce the trial evaluation, discuss its form and purpose and establish a pattern of practice for the future. Specifically, the following issues were raised:

- the rationale for the choice of target areas;
- data collection methods to be used;
- intended uses of the information collected.

During this meeting, staff were provided with supporting documentation.

Supporting documentation

The senior management team wished to ensure that staff were fully informed about the evaluation. A booklet ('Evaluation Policy 1990') was prepared and distributed to all staff as an interim policy statement and an *aide mémoire* of what was discussed in the full staff meeting. This document began with the following statement of principle on the school's view of evaluation.

An evaluation system should:

- be fair to all concerned and become an integrated part of school life
- lead to the collecting of information, based on sound methodology and educational research, which can suggest remedial measures; every effort should be made to avoid causing harm to the learning and teaching processes
- lead to the compilation of a report which is easily understood with due consideration given to all staff opinions in the follow-up processes
- be economic in its use of resources.

The document went on to provide:

- an outline of what would be evaluated;
- details of the evaluation team membership;
- what data collection methods would be used;
- the time-scale of activities;
- a description of how the data collected would be used for review purposes.

This description of the proposed data use included the following statements:

The final evaluation report will be made available to all teachers of the school. It will be a confidential report to the teaching staff of the school. If this final report be requested by officers of the Education Authority then the school will remain anonymous. The purpose of drawing up a final report is to:
- transfer and disseminate information to all members of staff
- encourage further action where necessary
- give status and validity to the evaluation process.

It is intended that the report be brief and practical. It is expected that follow-up processes will take place based on the information presented in the final report. The follow-up will be on a whole-school level and at faculty/departmental level, depending on the relevance of the issues raised. This will give purpose and value to the processes described in this policy focusing in particular on:
- review of the curriculum
- staff development
- planning developments for the future.

It is hoped that evaluation will play a central role within school, not only of the teaching and learning processes but also the decision-making structure of the school.

The instruments to be used for the four priority areas, the school's targets, and the action planned in relation to each objective and performance indicator were appended to the evaluation policy statement.

Implementation

Most of the data were collected during the beginning of May. However, where information from pupils was involved, the school decided to supplement this summative collection by two formative collections, one in October and the other in December. This was done for a number of reasons:

- the evaluation team was able to get first-hand experience of pupils' reaction to the questionnaires and modify them so as to make them more accessible to other pupils;
- it gave pupils a 'dry-run' to familiarise them with the idea of completing evaluation questionnaires; it was hoped this would help responses gathered in the summative evaluation during May to be more reliable;
- it enabled the evaluation team to chart development as the year progressed, with a view to taking action if necessary.

For both the formative and summative data collection from pupils, the questionnaires were completed during a pastoral period.

A few days before undertaking the summative data collection, the evaluation team met briefly to confirm the common approach which would be used in administering the evaluation instruments. The pupil questionnaires were given out to all Year 10 pupils during the pastoral period on the day before they were to be completed. Both the form tutor and another member of the evaluation team were present to ensure consistency in interpreting the questionnaires. The school comments:

> The intention . . . was to give pupils an opportunity to become familiar with the proformas and questions being posed. They were asked to discuss amongst themselves in order to bring to mind their past experiences on various occasions in recent months. This was an attempt to increase the reliability of pupil responses.

The following day, pupils were asked to complete the written questionnaires during the pastoral period. Although the questionnaires had been designed to be used anonymously, the school decided to ask pupils to put their names on their completed responses, principally so the evaluation team could follow up on any questionnaires which were not filled in correctly. Also, the school felt that pupil responses would be more reliable if they were identifiable. As it turned out, the follow-up was not necessary, even in the case of less able pupils. The school comments: 'Not one pupil from Year 10 was absent on 9 May 1991, and the data was collected from pupils easily enough.'

Dan yr Olwg had made considerable efforts to facilitate the data collection from pupils because other schools, where the instruments had already been trialled, had highlighted a number of problems in this respect. The school assumed that data collection from staff and documentary sources would be more straightforward, since this had been the experience of other schools which had already trialled the evaluation instruments.

Reporting and review

The co-ordinating deputy headteacher compiled a report on the basis of the data collected. He distributed it to all heads of faculties and departments late in May for discussion in faculty/departmental meetings as part of the school's annual review process. Shortly afterwards, the senior management team, together with the co-ordinators responsible for the four priority areas, met with an LEA officer to discuss the evaluation report. During this meeting, agreement was reached on the need for action in particular areas. This was followed by discussions between the co-ordinators for the priority areas and heads of faculties/departments to agree on specific details of future developments.

This evaluation exercise had also been used to trial the self-evaluation approach, and there was need to review the experiment. The co-ordinating deputy headteacher prepared a list of questions which were discussed during a full staff meeting in June 1991:

- Are the pupil questionnaires suitable for the children?
- Is the information collected relevant and useful?
- What use should be made of the information collected?
- What steps should we take to integrate self-evaluation into the whole of the school's work?
- How can the information be used to improve pupils' experiences in the classroom?

The school is currently moving forward to developing the interim statement into a whole-school evaluation policy, in the light of this trialling period.

GENERAL ISSUES

The case study cited above, in giving the experience of one secondary school, inevitably involves consideration of details which are specific to the particular circumstances and organisational structure of that school. None the less, it also highlights some of the general issues which will apply to all schools, primary and secondary. The following points emerge from this case study.

Vision

The school managers had a strong vision of what was to be achieved. Their commitment to sharing this vision was reflected both in producing an interim policy statement and in using staff meeting time for discussing evaluation.

Winning over staff

The school recognised that it would be crucial to allay staff fears and create a climate in which evaluation would not be frozen out through passive resistance.

They recognised that sharing their vision was only one element in this process. Another vital ingredient was the active involvement of a team of key staff through setting realistic targets, undertaking the data collection, and agreeing with colleagues the future action following review.

Staff development

Only one staff member, a deputy headteacher, had received formal training. For other staff to feel confident about implementing the evaluation, it was necessary for him to devote time to sharing some of the elements in that training with his team. (At this stage the school did not feel ready to replicate the full training programme.)

Action orientation

The central focus of the evaluation was developmental. It was therefore essential to ensure that the results of the evaluation were used to inform future action. The school therefore at the planning stage built in a dissemination strategy which was discussed with the whole staff in advance.

From pilot to extension

The school wanted to move forward from the trial and ensure that evaluation became embedded in all teachers' normal practice. All staff were therefore involved in discussion of how best to develop further the evaluation.

The school in the case study is still in the process of determining the next steps in extending its self-evaluation. The final chapter of this book describes some issues which schools may wish to consider for development in the longer term.

Chapter 8

An integrated approach to evaluation and review

The implicit theme of this book has been evaluation for school development and that is certainly the approach to evaluation we wish to encourage. Curricular evaluation and review should not exist in isolation and their long-term impact on school performance is likely to depend on how they are integrated with other forms of review.

We shall examine some of the issues relating to integration of review both within a school and also between schools and the LEA. It is not our intention to examine any of these issues in depth. Rather we hope that this chapter may stimulate discussion about the way forward in schools, following the training and initial trialling of a systematic approach to evaluation.

WHOLE-SCHOOL REVIEW

By and large, evaluation of schools, whether external or internal, has tended to focus on curricular issues. The 1986 and 1988 Education Acts legislate for the introduction of staff appraisal and financial management in the local manage-ment of schools. Clearly, these issues are interrelated: curriculum delivery and pupils' achievements are greatly affected by the quality of teaching and resources provided. Any school which seeks to use management information effectively for planning purposes will need to devise systems for integrating a review of:

- curriculum delivery and pupil outcomes;
- staff appraisal and development;
- use of finance and other material resources.

Systematic evaluation should start with the curriculum, since decisions relating to staff development and the use of material resources should be determined by curricular priorities. In planning for curriculum evaluation, a school will focus on the extent to which its development plans are being implemented. The data collected will inevitably be concentrated on teaching and learning processes and on pupil outcomes as evidenced by achievements, attitudes and behaviour. None the less, it is highly likely that at least some curriculum evaluation will involve consideration of staff development issues and resource deployment (see the examples given in Chapter 3, Figures 3.2 and 3.3). However, staff development issues are treated more systematically through staff appraisal, and issues relating to material resources through the school's financial systems.

In many schools, these three systems currently operate relatively independently of one another. It would make better sense for curriculum evaluation to be integrated with both staff appraisal and material resource management systems. This is most effectively achieved through the whole-school review process. As we indicated in Chapter 2, this review is not a single event but a series of structured discussions which culminate in informed decisions about future action. Although curricular evaluation, staff appraisal and material resource evaluation systems can operate in relative independence, it is crucial that information generated by all three be used in review and forward planning. This is illustrated diagrammatically in Figure 8.1.

Whole-school review is the hub of the process. Through this review, the effectiveness of the existing provision can be gauged, taking into account all the relevant, available information. As we indicated in Figure 2.4, review consists of both looking back and looking forward. Planning for the future should ideally encompass:

- identifying priority objectives, strategies and specific targets, that is, *curriculum planning*;
- earmarking the appropriate facilitators, to include both *staffing and material resource planning*.

This book has largely been devoted to a discussion of school evaluation with the focus on priority curriculum objectives. We now need to devote some space to staff appraisal issues and to material resource monitoring and evaluation.

STAFF APPRAISAL

As the DES has pointed out, 'it is important that appraisal is not done for its own sake but to be seen as a tool integral to the management of other initiatives and strategies' (DES 1989b). Its principal twin focuses are accountability and improving staff performance. Through both classroom or task observation and interview sessions, appraisers acquire a detailed knowledge of the appraisees' level of expertise and their development needs. They also acquire information about how effectively appraisees are teaching and managing and the extent to which these individuals are meeting particular curricular objectives. Clearly, pooling such information about individuals should help in constructing a picture of the school's teaching provision. None the less, data relating to specific individuals must be handled sensitively and with due consideration for maintaining confidentiality. For example, while headteachers have a responsibility to set out for governing bodies 'a summary of targets for actions for appraisees, decided at appraisal interviews, and progress in achieving past targets', this is subject to 'the need to avoid the attribution of targets to individuals' (DES/WO 1991, para. 65).

Figure 8.1 An integrated review system

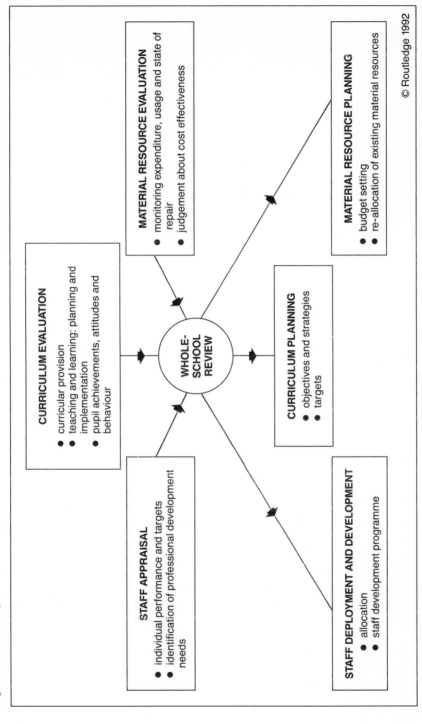

Likewise, individual teachers have the right to confidentiality in respect of their appraisal statement (DES/WO 1991, para. 55), and the persons who can have access to individual statements are delimited in the regulations. Further, individuals' rights under the Data Protection Act of 1984 must also be safeguarded. With the appropriate safeguards in place, aggregated data from appraisal interviews can and should be an invaluable source of reliable information to feed into the whole-school review.

The principal data collection methods for appraising include classroom or task observation and one-to-one interviews. Clearly, appraisers need to develop negotiation and observation skills to enable them to structure and manage such situations effectively (Poster and Poster, 1991). We suggested earlier in Chapter 3 that, when getting started on curriculum evaluation, schools would be well advised to limit the use of observation. However, once an appraisal system is established and accepted, and senior staff have developed classroom observation techniques, this data collection method is readily incorporated into curriculum evaluation.

The school also needs feedback on the efficacy of its management structures and lines of communication. Staff perceptions on how appropriate the present management systems and procedures are can be gleaned during the appraisal process. Likewise, senior managers can use their own appraisal as the opportunity to reflect on how effectively the school's management systems are operating. An external assessment is provided through the headteacher's management performance appraisal. As with information on individual classroom performance, data relating to management performance needs to be used sensitively. Nevertheless, a whole-school review is incomplete unless it considers management issues.

MATERIAL RESOURCE EVALUATION

Thus far, we have concentrated on evaluation in terms of effectiveness, with only limited mention of efficiency. A fully integrated evaluation and review system should embrace both. Some LEA inspectorates have already begun to look at the effect of resourcing decisions on pupils' education (McGee, 1991). With the advent of the local management of schools, governing bodies and headteachers have increased powers and responsibilities not only to ensure financial probity but also to get the best value they can from the available resources. This implies not only targeting resources to support the delivery of specific objectives, but also monitoring the actual expenditure and the use of equipment, together with assessing the state of repair of equipment and premises. Such information needs to be used as part of the whole-school review process. This should provide a sound basis on which to make assessments on past financial decisions, and inform qualitative judgements which have to be made about the relative merits of different financial proposals.

Figure 8.2 Interrelationships between various management processes at each operational level

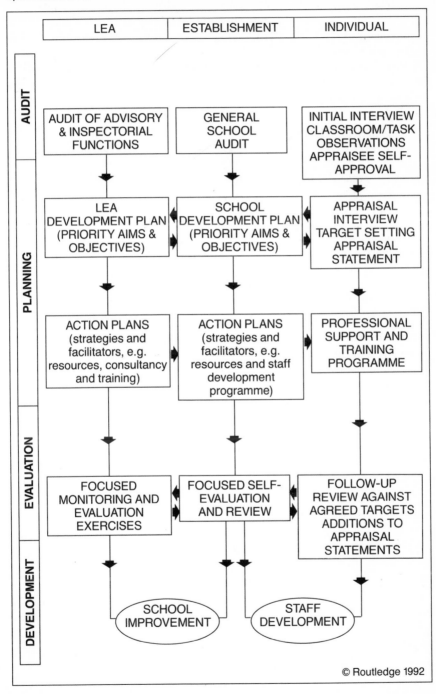

© Routledge 1992

SCHOOL/LEA REVIEW PARTNERSHIP

The school is required to report on its achievements to parents and governors. The LEA currently has the duty to monitor schools' implementation of the requirements of the 1988 Education Reform Act. It is in the interests of both to be mutually supportive.

There are clear parallels in planning, evaluation and review at LEA, school and individual teacher level. Each can benefit where there is a co-ordinated flow of information and purposeful interaction between mutually supportive agencies working towards common goals. For example, the school development plans should be both influenced by and influence the LEA development plans. In this way, what the LEA provides will be better matched to the schools' needs.

Likewise, where personal targets are agreed in the light of the school's curricular priorities, the professional development opportunities available are more likely to be embraced willingly by staff. So too with evaluation, appraisal and review, pooling information and insights provides a more comprehensive overview, which should lead to better informed decisions at all levels and hence to both school and staff improvement. This is illustrated diagrammatically in Figure 8.2.

CONCLUSION

The scenarios painted in Figures 8.1 and 8.2 will be, for most schools, long-term aims. At present, managing delegated budgets, establishing effective staff appraisal, and embedding systematic curricular evaluation are still in the process of development in most schools. What we have tried to do in this book is to offer practical guidance on getting started with curricular evaluation, together with a vision of how this could be linked with appraisal and resource management in due course.

References

Bolam, R. (1987) 'What is effective INSET?', paper presented to NFER Annual Conference, 1987, Windsor: NFER (mimeo).

Clift, P.S., Nuttall, D.L. and McCormick, R. (1987) *Studies in School Self-Evaluation*, London: Falmer.

Cohen, L. and Manion, C. (1989) *Research Methods in Education*, London: Routledge.

DES (1989a) *School Indicators for Internal Management: An Aide Mémoire*, Publications Despatch Centre, London: Department of Education and Science.

DES (1989b) HMI Report *Developments in the Appraisal of Teachers*, London: Department of Education and Science.

DES/WO (1991) *School Teacher Appraisal*, Circular No. 21/91, London: Department of Education and Science/Circular No. 43/91, Cardiff: Welsh Office, Education Department.

McGee, P. (1991) 'The quality contract', *Education*, 27 September 1991.

Poster, C. and Poster, D. (1991) *Teacher Appraisal*, London: Routledge.

Tipple, C. (1989) 'Measuring achievement', *Education*, 29 September 1989.

Further reading

We have purposely avoided providing lists of citations in the text since we wished to provide the reader with a self-contained manual. However, the interested reader may find it helpful to have some indications of areas for further reading.

This further reading list does not claim to be exhaustive – far from it – but may be of some use to the reader who wishes to pursue some of the issues discussed in the book.

Bell, J. (1987) *Doing your Research Project*, Milton Keynes: Open University Press.

CIPFA (1988) *Performance Indicators for Schools. A Contribution to the Debate*, London: Chartered Institute of Public Finance and Accountancy.

Davidson, G., Howlett, K. and Parsons, C. (1991) *Evaluation for Schools and Colleges. A Staff Development Manual*, Lancaster: Framework Press.

Fitz-Gibbon, C.T. (ed.) (1990) *Performance Indicators*, BERA Dialogues No. 2, Clevedon: Multilingual Matters.

Hargreaves, D.H., Hopkins, D., Leask, M., Conolly, J. and Robinson, P. (1989) *Planning for School Development: Advice to Governors, Headteachers and Teachers*, London: HMSO.

Hopkins, D. (1989) *Evaluation for School Development*, Milton Keynes: Open University Press.

McCormick, R. and James, M. (1989) *Curriculum Evaluation in Schools*, London: Routledge.

Morris, M. and Twitchin, R. (1990) *Evaluating Flexible Learning: A User's Guide*, Slough: NFER.

Murphy, R. and Torrance, H. (eds) (1987) *Evaluating Education: Issues and Methods*, London: Harper & Row.

Rogers, G. and Badham, L. (1990) 'Partners in evaluation', *Education*, 3 August 1990.

Society of Chief Inspectors and Advisers (1989) *Evaluating the Educational Achievements of Schools and Colleges: The Use of Indicators*, Discussion Paper No. 2, SCIA.

Skilbeck, M. (ed.) (1984) *Evaluating the Curriculum in the Eighties*, London: Hodder & Stoughton.

Wilcox, B. (1992) *Time-Constrained Evaluation*, London: Routledge.

Index